My heart in hiding | Stirred for a bird,— the achieve of, the mastery of the thing!
— Gerard Manley Hopkins

ROBERT BATEMAN
BIRDS

Foreword by
PETER MATTHIESSEN
Text by Kathryn Dean

FIREFLY BOOKS

A FIREFLY BOOKS / MADISON PRESS BOOK

A FIREFLY BOOK

Published by Firefly Books Ltd. 2018

First printing

Publisher Cataloging-in-Publication Data (U.S.)

Library of Congress Control Number: 2018942029

Library and Archives Canada Cataloguing in Publication

A CIP record for this title is available from Library and Archives Canada

Published in the United States by
Firefly Books (U.S.) Inc.
P.O. Box 1338, Ellicott Station
Buffalo, New York 14205

Published in Canada by
Firefly Books Ltd.
50 Staples Avenue, Unit 1
Richmond Hill, Ontario L4B 0A7

Printed in China

This title was produced by:
Madison Press Books
31 Adelaide Street East, PO Box 608
Toronto, Ontario, Canada M5C 2J8
madisonpressbooks.com

 We acknowledge the financial support of the Government of Canada

Robert Bateman 2001 ©

For Roger Tory
Peterson, the
father of the field
guide, who opened
a window to the
creatures of the
natural world so
that we could know,
understand, and
protect them.

TABLE OF CONTENTS

FOREWORD

I first met Bob Bateman in Seattle at a celebration of the International Snow Leopard Trust, of which he is a trustee and supporter; I met him next in 1998, with his lovely wife, Birgit, in Tierra del Fuego, from where we were embarking to South Georgia Island and the Antarctic Peninsula as field guides of a wildlife safari expedition led by our mutual friend, the ornithologist Victor Emanuel. Since then, we have shared a number of these adventures—a sailing voyage through islands of the southern Caribbean, seeking rare parrots in their disappearing habitats high in the mountains; an old-fashioned *caravanserai* on the railroads of central India—"the Royal Palace on Wheels"—which took us to four of the last strongholds of the Indian tiger as well as to such exotic places as Old Delhi, Kujaraho, and the Taj Mahal; and most recently a return to Antarctica, this time on a twenty-six-day voyage from Tasmania to Macquarie Island and the emperor penguin colonies in the Ross Sea.

On all of these trips, of course, I had the pleasure of observing Robert Bateman in the field—not only his painstaking observation and execution of the swift expert notebook sketches, but the daily labor of lugging tripods and heavy camera equipment in and out of small boats in rough weather, across swamps and up mountainsides, or in tropical heat and dust—the endless taking down and setting up of technical equipment in difficult conditions and/or trying circumstances, not to obtain rare photographs that might be marketed in reward of so much effort (though his photographs, and Birgit's, too, are of the highest quality) but simply to record those exquisite details of color and texture, those idiosyncratic quirks of posture and behavior, that will later emerge so authentically and beautifully in the finished work.

Bateman's philosophy of art (and its underlying conservation ethic) are forcefully expressed in his own introduction to this book—no need to muddy his ideas with mine. His picture notes, too, are sharply observed and require no comment. But I would like to express great admiration for the originality and boldness of certain pieces in this volume, such as the grotesque pair of giant petrels harassing the leucistic gentoo penguin, which is almost Gothic in its strangeness, yet entirely authentic in ornithological detail. And the magnificent Snow-Wreath—the Siberian crane—in a stylized threat posture much more difficult to fix on canvas than the standard poses (and uninspired colors) in what passes ordinarily for "wildlife art."

Another challenge that his vision set him is a foreshortened view of a preening red-crowned crane (right), which was used on the jacket of the British edition of our book on cranes—*The Birds of Heaven*—published last year. One of the finest bird renderings I have ever seen, it is almost mandarin in its attention to plumage texture and exquisite detail. And, of course, Bob Bateman has long since transcended the limited genre of wildlife art, which is why his works are hung in art museums and private collections rather than club rooms, steak houses, and hook-and-bullet bars. It is why he is spoken of around the world in the same breath as Bruno Liljefors and those few other interpreters of the natural world who may be regarded as true painters and creative artists.

—*Peter Matthiessen*
Sagaponack, New York, May 2002

INTRODUCTION

A chickadee started me on a lifetime as a birder. I had seen pictures of them in books and knew about their black bibs, but I paid little attention to them—until one November afternoon when I was eight years old. On that brisk, late autumn day, I was exploring a lane in the farm fields north of Toronto when I was stopped in my tracks by a lively ball of fluff hopping from twig to twig in a leafless hedge. I'd always thought a chickadee was more or less like a house sparrow, but this tiny bird's white cheeks, black cap, and upside-down gymnastics gave it away immediately—and the agile climber charmed the cold right out of the afternoon.

That chickadee turned me into a hunter—equipped not with a gun, but with my eyes and ears. Immersed in the natural lore of Ernest Thompson Seton's *Two Little Savages*, I spent hours stalking my prey in the tangled ravine behind my parents' house, inching through the vines and bushes as stealthily as a fox. It was an adventure and a mystery—but the mystery verged on frustration because I had no decent bird book to help me identify what I had seen. Salvation finally arrived on my twelfth birthday when my mother gave me the birder's bible—Roger Tory Peterson's *Field Guide to the Birds*. Before long, I was joined by friends who would drop everything to look for a catbird mewing in the wild-grape jungle or a hummingbird swinging like a crazy pendulum among the plum blossoms. We were caught by the birds.

Now, in the twenty-first century, millions of people have been enthralled by the chase. Birders are part of a global village, complete with hotlines and websites, and their activities contribute over $10 billion to the economy of the United States alone. It's not surprising. Of all the denizens of the wild, birds are the flashiest and the easiest to see. They tantalize us with their dazzling and subtle plumage, their ethereal and raucous calls, and their diverse behavior. An ostrich can disembowel you with a kick; a robin's song can melt your heart with memories. Yet the lives of birds are elusive. They grace us with a few moments of beauty, then sail away through spaces of green and blue on voyages we will never take.

There is something refreshing in learning about a living creature so removed from our own daily interests. Perhaps that's why birders are such a contented lot. One psychiatrist I met had even concluded that birders were among the most mentally healthy people in the world. And it's true that their joy and comradeship are legendary. They can go for years without seeing each other, but as soon as they meet again, it's as if no time has passed. My birding friends and I can stand long periods of separation and pick up right where we left off as we hunt for hooded warblers on the shores of Lake Erie during the May migration season or make our way along slippery jungle trails.

But my most valued birding companion is my wife, Birgit. She started with a baptism of fire at the Niagara Gorge one autumn weekend—a complete beginner, surrounded by hundreds of serious birders and thousands of gulls. The air over the gorge looked like a mass of reeling confetti—mostly white and gray, but with subtle distinctions of bill and leg color, and bits of black. Birgit rose to the occasion and spotted Bonapartes and Sabine gulls, ring-billed and mew gulls—and the most elusive of them all, a straggler from Europe known as the little gull. She fell in love with the challenge.

As I have painted the birds that appear in the following pages, I have viewed them as an artist—blending colors to find the exact vermilion hue of the scarlet tanager or angling the feathers of the yellow-crowned night heron to show their complex geometry. In the process, I've created not a field guide or a reference book, but a portfolio of sketches and paintings, as well as a field diary of the enriching hours I have spent with Birgit, observing birds on many continents. I hope these images will remind many more people of similar days when they have hiked through the woods or boated down rivers, watching for a particular flash of color or listening for a series of notes that could reveal the presence of a hermit thrush.

In the theater of nature, birds perform daily activities like our own, but with unusual and often entertaining variations. We identify with some parts of their lives and recognize the fact that we do not exist in isolation. Unfortunately, however, we sometimes come home from our birding expeditions and forget that we are not alone on the stage of the earth. We have the privilege of protecting the birds that share the world with us, but we often neglect this pleasant duty. Our lifestyles have become so dependent on exploiting the natural world that even as we carry out our day-to-day activities, we are destroying birds and their habitats at a faster rate than any generation before us—and threatening our own survival at the same time. It is predicted that over the next hundred years we will lose 1,200 species of birds—or one in eight. They will be gone forever, and without them, the lives of our descendants will be bleaker. But we should not despair.

If I have one hope, it is that everyone will take a closer look at the natural world, and in my view, birds are the place to start. Tens of thousands of people and hundreds of organizations around the world are actively engaged not only in appreciating birds, but in joining the battle to save their habitats and stem the tide of destruction. These hardworking groups always need more members and more support. When people ask me what they can do to help, I always tell them to join up and get involved.

The birds in this book are an inheritance we have received from previous generations. If we combine our skills and resources, we will be able to pass this natural legacy on to our grandchildren's grandchildren. There is no cause more worthy than this.

Robert Bateman
Salt Spring Island,
British Columbia
May 2002

AT HOME ON SALT SPRING ISLAND

I've always wanted to live by the ocean, but Salt Spring Island, off the coast of British Columbia, offers much more than just a seaside view. On the hill behind our back garden are remnants of mossy coastal forest, around the house the microclimate is Mediterranean—sunny and dry—and when we walk down to the ocean, we pass through a zone that's lush and full of life: clams lie in the sand, and purple starfish climb up a cliff when the tide comes in. Because of the generous climate and the diversity of life zones, we are graced with a wide variety of birdlife—from violet-green swallows to harlequin ducks.

The Gulf Islands are also bald eagle country. I knew these raptors liked to perch on dead trees, but the edge of our property that faces the sea was originally open and bare—so I decided to create a more welcoming habitat. I hunted around for a suitable snag, found a dead cedar complete with branches for perching, and "planted" it in cement in the perfect viewing spot from both the bedroom and the studio.

Within a couple of weeks, a bald eagle carrying something heavy came flying along and headed straight for the tree. After a lot of flapping, it made a perfect landing—right on the perch I'd designed for it. The bird was carrying a big piece of fish skin, and it sat there eating its meal in a leisurely way. Although eagles do not raise their young on our property, I saw this nest (left) at another location on Salt Spring Island.

Bald Eagle

The otters that live under our house love holding sliding parties when it snows, but those frozen days are hard for the black-tailed deer. One winter, a yearling failed in its search for food and died on our garden steps, leaving me to puzzle over what to do with the little body. The ground was too hard to bury it, so in the end, I decided to turn the deer into a bird feeder. I slit it open and placed it on the rocks by the ocean, where it could be seen from the studio and the bedroom. Before long, we had visits from crows, ravens, and at least three different bald eagles, including the one shown below. The deer fed the hungry birds, then made its final contribution to the cycle of life as food for the crabs and fish below the tide line.

The armor-like plumage of eagles like this one has always intrigued me as an artist. Unlike the fur of mammals, which reveals the curve of every muscle, the hundreds of individual feathers on the eagle's body overlap to create a tough outer covering.

Great Blue Heron

In the morning, the water at our dock is usually flat, with barely a ripple. The color may be lead-gray, pink, or gold during most seasons, but in summer it is opalescent blue. That is when an elegant great blue heron sometimes appears, beating in low across the water, the bird and his reflection looking like a letter W and an M nearly touching at the surface. Over half the heron's length consists of head and neck. When he spots a fish, his gracefully curved neck straightens out at lightning speed, and with a toss of his head, he swallows his prey. Then the heron stands still again, assuming his role as a statue, waiting for another meal to appear (right).

In calmer moments, great blue herons preen themselves, using their bills to pluck specialized down feathers, which crumble into a powder. The bird rubs its head and neck through this residue, rolling the slime on its feathers into clumps. Then the heron brushes off the accumulated grit with one swipe of its claws. Clean and ready for a new feeding foray, the bird takes flight, moving through the air with powerful strokes of its enormous wings.

The great blue heron, affectionately known to birders as the GBH, is the largest and most widespread of all North American herons, frequenting marshes and tidal flats all over the continent and south into Central America and the Caribbean.

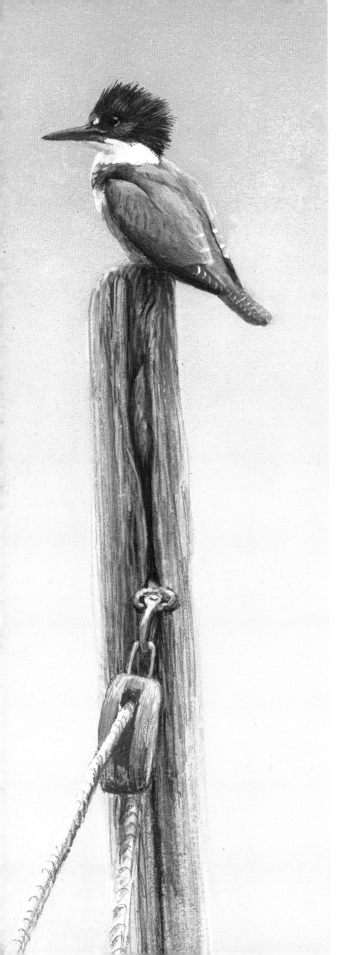

Belted Kingfisher

Sometimes our resident kingfisher (left) leaves her fishing perch when the heron arrives. But other days, she holds her ground on the clothesline post we use to launch our boat. I painted her in that stance, poised and ready to dive into the water after a small fish. Her hunting skill is enhanced by extra color-perceiving cone receptors, and she is a precision diver, adjusting her aim to compensate for the refraction of light from the water's surface.

Rufous Hummingbird

In spring, a fir twig not much thicker than a fishing line is strong enough to bear the weight of this rufous hummingbird when he perches just inches from our bedroom window (right). I've never found the hummingbirds' lichen and cobweb nest, but I know they build one every year, because the male always flies at us when we venture out onto the kitchen deck. This scrappy jewel posed so well that I had time to capture him on his delicate perch.

Every year, I am amazed by the early return of these migrants. The males fly north before the females in late March—about the time the wild currants begin to show their crimson flowers. But their tropical colors are only a prelude to more spectacular displays: when the females arrive a short time later, both sexes are transformed into kaleidoscopes of changing hues as the dizzying courtship flights begin. The hummingbird suitor rockets straight up into the air, then dives right down again, hovering beside the one he is trying to impress. The burnished orange of his throat is one attraction—a shimmering display created as light refracts from the bird's multi-faceted throat feathers.

Like a gift, the rufous-throated hummingbird is suddenly there, perched on a light twig or sipping nectar from tubular flowers. As it hovers, its wings whir so quickly that it uses seven times more oxygen than when it is at rest.

Varied Thrush

When winter snows have covered the mountains and food has become scarce even in the valleys, the varied thrushes alight in our garden, foraging for fruit still hanging from the trees.

Nicknamed the Alaska robin, this bird behaves like its namesake, but its markings are much more interesting to me as an artist. The male's plumage is marked by geometrical patterns of orange encased in dusky bluish-gray, its wings are layered with orange-gold epaulets, and a black necklace drapes neatly around the base of its throat. The male in the painting at left has visited our evergreen arbutus before and has already eaten most of the fruit. But in a few seconds he may flit down to the end of the branch and discover the red berries hidden under the snow.

Junco

Snow comes only rarely to Salt Spring Island, but when it arrives, the world outside our window becomes an enchanted place. On one of those mornings, a dark-eyed junco alighted on the Garry oak and perched there with its feathers plumped up against the cold (right). The dark-eyed juncos of the west were once known as "Oregons," but several years ago, scientists put them in the same category as the eastern "slate-colored" subspecies and gave them all their new name—much to the dismay of some birders, who blamed the ornithological bureaucracy for the loss of one bird from their life lists.

White-Crowned Sparrow

I learned the song of the white-crowned sparrow during my first summer working in the Arctic. Since then, I've often heard these birds singing on the bough of the Douglas fir outside our bedroom window as they pause in their migration south to Mexico (left). Their notes rise in a slightly plaintive crescendo, and they often sing at night.

To remember the song of a particular species, birders sometimes make up phrases that have a similar sound. The white-throated sparrow, for instance, sings, "*O sweet Canada, Canada, Canada,*" though some prefer the American version: "*O Sam Peabody, Peabody, Peabody.*" The white-crowned sparrow, on the other hand, sings, "*Poor Jojo wet his pants.*" Many songbirds have unique accents in different parts of the continent, but the white-crowned sparrow beside our house comes close enough to singing "Jojo's song" to be recognizable.

Spotted Towhee

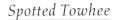

In the painting above, I have tried to capture the subtle changes that signal the coming of winter. The bold markings, medieval hood, and blood-red eye of the spotted towhee are half eclipsed by the briar's smoky red branch and luminescent leaves. But those vestiges of summer are marked by decay. One leaf edge is crumpled and bronzed, and others are turning from yellow-green to purplish-red.

Violet-Green Swallow

Springtime sneaks up on the Gulf Islands, starting in January, when signs of change gradually appear on the landscape. An important one for me is the arrival of a pair of violet-green swallows fluttering and conversing in gurgling twitters at the birdhouse right outside my studio window. Their iridescent green and reddish-purple backs glisten as they sail out into space to land on the big eagle tree or a sprig of lichen-covered Garry oak (above).

These swallows like to nest in tree cavities—often taking over deserted woodpecker holes or building on an unused bluebird's nest. But clear-cutting has eliminated whole tracts of their breeding grounds, so the swallows are forced to look for other places to raise their young. In their case, birdhouses are a decided benefit.

California Quail

Even as far north as Salt Spring, we are often delighted by the sounds of California quails bustling beneath the trees (left). They come to the feeder outside my studio, gabbling to each other as they creep along the ground, with one male always standing sentinel. Their stippled white markings and teardrop-shaped crests make them look like ornately costumed Victorians at a banquet. This plumage is appropriate, since they are very social birds—except when they pair off to nest during mating season. By fall, we frequently see them in coveys of twenty to forty, feeding on berries and picking up the grit they use to grind up seeds in their gizzards.

Ruffed Grouse

For centuries, mainstream western art portrayed wildlife like the grouse as quarry or prey, not depicting the creatures as beings in their own right as I prefer to do. However, paintings by the old masters showing birds "after the hunt" are often interesting from an artistic point of view. Following in that tradition, I have painted the ruffed grouse at right in a strong side light to accent the eloquence of its feather patterns.

Like many ground-dwelling and low-flying birds, this grouse was killed in a collision with a car. But many others disappear every year at the hands of game hunters. In the bad old days of unrestricted hunting, edible birds like the grouse were destroyed by the hundreds of thousands by market hunters, endangering many species and making some, like the passenger pigeon, extinct. In a few New England states, hunters were once paid bounties to reduce the grouse population and to stop the birds from eating the buds of fruit trees.

Hunting is no longer needed to provide food in many parts of the world, but it has survived as a recreational activity. Though I am not part of those circles, I appreciate the work of many hunting organizations and governments, which pour millions of dollars into wildlife management and habitat protection, to the benefit of all species.

Robert Bateman

Goldeneye

As winter approaches, the goldeneyes come flying in, looking for refuge on our saltwater shores. They nest near woodland lakes and rivers, but when freeze-up arrives, they migrate to the ocean's edge, where they can forage for mollusks and tiny fish. We saw this pair (left) diving for food and gliding along the satiny water as if they were connected by an invisible thread. The male's stark white cheek patches and breast formed a sunny counterpoint to the female's dark brown plumage and pale-striped bill.

Hooded Merganser

Like players in a medieval pageant with ribboned tunics and regal crests, these hooded mergansers (below) move through calm waters in their stately, secretive way. Although they are never here in large numbers, a pair of them are almost always working the waters near the cliffs on our shoreline. Sometimes in the spring, a few pairs appear in a small flotilla, and we are treated to some nuptial displays—including crest-flaring performances by the males. Shortly thereafter, they disappear from our view and make their way inland where they lay their eggs and raise their young.

Deceptively gray and nondescript from a distance, the male harlequin duck transforms himself into a piebald swatch of slate blue, white, and chestnut when he comes up close. The female looks more neatly tailored with her white ear patch and brownish grays. We saw this pair (right) as they were about to dive for crabs and periwinkles, using a half-decayed fir log as a springboard. But both stayed long enough for me to sketch their symmetrical pose before they plunged into the steely waters, uttering their mouse-like squeaks. About half the size of mallards, they must feed frequently to keep up their energy.

Glaucous-Winged, Thayer's, and Mew Gulls

Birgit and I slowed the canoe as we neared Jackson Rocks. These craggy islets cover less than half an acre, but they provide a refuge for many seabirds and migrating flocks. They're part of the North Pacific's intertidal zone, which has the greatest variety of plant and animal species of all the temperate seashores in the world. Bladderwrack, barnacles, and mollusks attach themselves to its solid edges, attracting a whole crowd of birds. Gulls, oystercatchers, and sandpipers wait for the tide to retreat, leaving fish, crabs, and mussels stranded and ready to be eaten.

We drifted toward the rocks and raised our binoculars, and, as so often happens, there was nothing to be seen on the nearest promontory—but the southern point was alive with gulls (left). Although the birds tend to segregate themselves by species, we had to look carefully to identify their differences. Glaucous-winged gulls have frosty gray and white wingtips with pink legs and a red dot on the lower mandible. Thayer's gulls are almost the same, but their wingtips are black and white. Mew gulls, on the other hand, have yellowish-green legs, puffy heads, and more slender bills, without the red dot—but like the Thayer's, their wingtips are also black and white.

I must add a note of caution: recently experts have claimed that many so-called Thayer's gulls are actually hybrids of herring gulls, glaucous-winged gulls, or western gulls. Nature is not only more complicated than we know, it is more complicated than we can perhaps ever know.

Black Turnstone

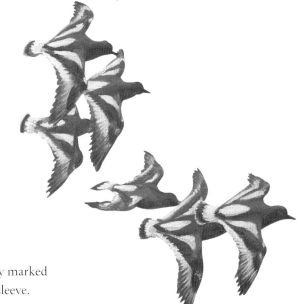

Our canoe drifted through the mist, but the subdued tones of the day were interrupted as Jackson Rocks suddenly came to life. Here and there, flashes of black and white wings rose from the islet, and seconds later, the ragged surface of the rocks erupted into a chorus of shrill twittering. Dozens of black turnstones flew into the air, flashing and wheeling as if they were a single bird, only to land a short distance away (overleaf).

The first black turnstones always swoop south from their Arctic breeding grounds in July, and by late fall our Pacific coastline is awash with the migrants, picking their way skillfully over offshore rocks in search of insects and mollusks. Unlike many species, these birds come to the same wintering grounds every year.

Ruddy turnstones have astonishing red and black jigsaw markings. Their clearly marked patterns curve from the base of the tail to the tip of the wing like gores on a raglan sleeve.

When shorebirds fly, they offer a constantly changing set of visual thrills (above). Their flashing patterns are visible from above and below, and the flock etches sweeping contours across the sky as each bird is mysteriously prompted to turn in unison with the others.

IN THE PRIBILOFS

The sheer rockfaces of the Pribilof Islands—north of the Aleutians in the Bering Sea—could be called Alcid heaven. As part of a wildlife tour we flew to one of the islands, where the weather is usually so harsh that the local Aleut residents told us we should have been there the year before, when "summer was on a Thursday!" But that July day, the sun was out. Around us were buildings that showed the influence of the Russian fur traders who first established this community in the eighteenth century (below).

As we approached the island's edges, the sounds reached us first, followed soon afterwards by the unforgettable smell. The chowdery combination of fish, salt, guano, and broken eggs carried me back to days I'd spent in gannet colonies on Quebec's Gaspé Peninsula and among crowds of penguins in Antarctica. At the cliffs, we either crouched or lay right down on the turf and leaned over the edge, and were transported into another world—a chaos of smell and sight as well as sound. The cries, shrieks, and growls of the cliff's inhabitants were underscored by the crashing surf churning so far below that I could not synchronize sound to sight. The air was thick with birds and the rocks were encrusted with them.

Like tuxedoed flying penguins, the murres dominated the wider ledges, resting, roosting, squabbling, adjusting, launching into space, and madly backpedaling to land. The kittiwakes twisted and dived and performed pirouettes apparently just for the joy of showing off their skills. And all the while they were screaming their name: "*Kittiwake, Kittiwake, Kittiwake.*" It was a world of reeling, raucous life on inches of rock.

The lichen-covered rockfaces of the Pribilof Islands (right) are home to nearly all of the world's approximately 250,000 red-legged kittiwakes—sociable birds that are in constant conversation with each other (seen at top). Their living arrangements may look random, but the kittiwakes and their neighbors operate within a strict hierarchy. The common murres (at bottom left and above), thick-billed murres (at bottom right), and clown-faced tufted puffins each have their own locations on the cliff, depending on their size and needs. Murres, for instance, will tend to nest on large, lower ledges, while kittiwakes can adapt to narrow spaces higher on the cliff.

Horned and Tufted Puffins

As I looked over the cliff, one tufted puffin appeared from behind a rock ledge and peered back. We played a few rounds of this game until the puffin decided I could safely be ignored. Then I settled down to sketch him and the nearby horned puffins, and the painting at left began to evolve.

Slightly larger than their Atlantic cousins, tufted puffins (bottom left) have white Kabuki-actor faces and yellow plumes above and behind their eyes. In breeding season, their bills are a palimpsest of red, yellow, and sometimes even green—though, Cinderella-like, they turn to a dull reddish-brown by summer. But in this painting, the triangular shape of the tufted's bill became the dominant pattern—repeated in the rock and in the faces of the horned puffin pair (top left). Rockface colonies provide a seemingly endless supply of geometric combinations, and I've tried to capture a few of those here.

Parakeet, Crested, and Least Auklets

On another ledge sat the puffins' cousins—crested, least, and parakeet auklets, looking like a troupe of cartoon characters (right). The slate black of the crested auklets blended in smoothly with the tones of the volcanic rock, but their brilliant orange beaks and operatic crests betrayed their camouflage. On the rocks to their right, the least auklets stared at me with intense curiosity, looking like oversized baby robins with button eyes and webbed feet. A lone parakeet auklet, (right foreground) completed the scene.

TREELINE AND TUNDRA

When we think of the Far North, we often imagine blinding-white snow and barren wastes. These are elements of life in the world's polar regions, but summer does eventually reach the regions to the north, when the tundra is transformed into an extravagant palette of color and activity.

I had the privilege of entering this world one summer when I did fieldwork with my friend Bristol Foster. He was studying a rare species of vole at the treeline, near Churchill, Manitoba, where stunted spruce grow among the glacial debris and walls of boulders shelter hidden meadows. One day as we were crossing the lichen-textured tundra, we heard a lyrical whistle and knew we'd come upon a golden plover. Their gold-and-black speckled coloring blends in so well with the mottled terrain and low-growing bushes that you almost always hear them before you see them. Moving slowly ahead, we scoured every patch of ground, hoping to find a nest—and finally saw the female (above) fly up at my approach. On that first discovery,

we remained only a short while and set a twig in the ground to mark the spot. If we'd lingered, the mother would have stayed away so long that the eggs would have chilled or a predator may have noticed the commotion and raided the nest.

When we returned some time later, we were surprised to see that, in spite of our caution, the eggs had completely disappeared. I stared at the ground in disbelief. There wasn't even any depression to show where the nest had been. Then our eyes caught an emerging pattern—revealing four tiny chicks, right between my feet! Their camouflage was so effective that I could easily have stepped right on them without noticing (left).

Near Churchill, even tall species like spruce are stunted by permafrost and sculpted by the ice-laced winds that blow off Hudson Bay. The lesser yellowlegs to the right is perched on one of these weather-torn trees, whose lopsided branch formation acts as a natural compass. The prevailing north winds have prevented much growth on the north side of the spruce, so it's obvious that the fuller branches are reaching south. The yellowlegs is pointed toward the higher Arctic, facing the wind.

Robert Bateman 2001

Western Sandpiper

On a trip to Alaska's west coast in 1983, we joined the final leg of a pan–North American birding marathon which reproduced a famous trip made thirty years earlier by North America's birding guru, Roger Tory Peterson, and British ornithologist James Fisher. We were at Chevak, in the Yukon River Delta—home to the emperor goose, the rare spectacled eider duck, and so many Arctic flying pests that our meals of boiled pork chops always came with a side order of stewed mosquitoes. The Yukon River Delta was also the nesting ground of the sparrow-sized Western sandpiper. Male Western sandpipers do much of the nesting work—digging several scrapes on the dry, shrubby parts of the delta and letting the female (below) choose her preferred abode. The chicks are precocial—that is, they are feathered and ready to leave the nest soon after hatching. Unfortunately, Western sandpiper populations are in decline, since many mud flats on their Pacific coast migratory routes—including those of San Francisco and Panama—have been polluted by sewage or industrial contaminants.

Long-Tailed Jaeger

Finding a nest can be one of the most rewarding experiences a birder can have—but it's not always safe. While we were at Chevak, I came across the nest of the bird that the Inuit call *Isunngaq*. I didn't have long to study my discovery. Through the cool blue skies streamed one of the most aggressive parents I have ever encountered near a nest. It was the long-tailed jaeger (left) coming in for a landing—right on my head. Its streaming tail feathers gave away its identity from a fair distance, but I had to move quickly to make sure I wasn't clawed. At another nesting site, an infuriated jaeger with a Robin Hood–like mask once took off my hat—but that was better than feeling its hooked beak and sharp toes sink through my hair!

Snow Goose and Common Eider

Being on an Arctic breeding ground in summer is like witnessing the beginning of life itself. Wherever you turn, in every square inch of available space, young birds are being nurtured or hatched. I once enjoyed this exuberant experience as I did fieldwork for another scientist friend, also near Churchill, Manitoba—this time in a snow goose colony. I spent most of my days wading through the clear amber waters of a delta, checking every islet for eggs. There were many hundreds of pairs in the colony, and our job was to tag the newly hatched birds so they could be tracked for genetic and behavioral information. You could always tell when a chick was about to appear because you could hear it chipping away at the inside of the eggshell. And you always knew who the parents were because they made a continual racket until their nest was left in peace (right).

Snow geese were not the only birds nesting, courting, and feeding among the tundra hummocks and slowly meandering rivulets. Common eiders, Arctic terns, red-necked phalaropes, and parasitic jaegers all added to the melee. The male eiders were displaying on their territory and making loud, cow-like sounds. Others flew toward the open water like chunky two-toned wedges (below), while the females (above) stayed on their lichen-, seaweed-, and down-filled nests. These brooding places are like puddles of feathers that seem to have no more substance than air but are exceptionally warm. That's why the down has traditionally been used as stuffing for bedding—though this fact was of no benefit to the explorer Samuel Hearne when he came to the mouth of the Churchill River in the late eighteenth century. He observed, in his journals, that there were too few eider ducks in the vicinity to make it worthwhile to collect their plumes.

Short-Eared Owl

Unlike many owls, short-eareds prefer open spaces like the prairie and the tundra (left). They are generally quiet birds, but at times they can be flamboyant or ferocious. To avoid detection, they often pretend to be dead, and when they are surprised at their nests, they bark and squeal. During courtship, the male performs aerial displays that are unusual for an owl—shooting up into the air with strong wingbeats, often as high as six hundred to one thousand feet.

When we were working at Churchill, we found a nest of short-eared chicks, including one that was much smaller than its siblings (above). Most birds wait until all their eggs are laid before starting to incubate, giving each of the chicks an equal chance at survival. But owls begin to brood as soon as the first egg is laid, so the first offspring hatches sooner than the others and has a head start on life. The last one to be born might never catch up with its older, larger, and more aggressive siblings and often dies because it cannot compete for food. Some larger first-born birds—including eagles—make a pre-emptive strike, killing the younger sister or brother to eliminate the competition altogether. This behavior is called Cainism, after the biblical character who killed his younger brother.

ABOVE LARCH VALLEY

In that world of cliffs and constant wind, the air had a presence we could not feel at sea level. Maybe it was because the gap between us and the next mountain was roughly fifteen miles wide. Starting at Moraine Lake near Banff, we'd climbed the steep switchbacks to Larch Valley and had finally come to a high saddle where pine and birch clung to the mountainsides, twisted and dwarfed like natural bonsai.

Suddenly there was a movement in a nearby jumble of lichen-covered boulders. It was a hoary marmot—the first one I'd ever seen. I crept closer to the silver-furred animal and was surprised that it let me come near enough to see the gleam in its eye (above). Then, just as abruptly as it had appeared, the marmot uttered a whistling cry and dived back into its burrow. Only at that moment did I notice a distant roar, like the sound of a jet plane cutting through the sky. I turned to see a golden eagle, wings folded, speeding past the marmot's perch and into the abyss below the ridge.

Golden Eagle

Shortly before this large raptor (right) landed, he'd probably been zooming along at a rate of about forty or fifty miles per hour, gliding with the winds to reach this speed. Such a fast-moving bird could easily overheat, so, like an engine, the golden eagle comes equipped with his own cooling system—the surface muscles attached to his skin separate his body feathers to let some heat escape. The shock of hitting the rockface would also be fatal if not for the eagle's special landing gear. Powerful muscles set high up on his legs, near the body's center of gravity, absorb the force of impact.

Raven

As we continued our trek among the wind-sculpted trees, the silence was broken by a demanding, guttural croak offstage to the left—evidence that a raven was in the vicinity. That day, we only heard its call, but if it had appeared, we might have seen this largest member of the crow family indulging in wild acrobatics—hurtling through the air, diving, turning upside down, and twirling around and around. And if we had walked too close to the raven's nest, we could have been pelted with rocks, since this bird is one of the few that has learned how to use tools.

Scientists have theorized that ravens became crafty over the centuries as they learned how to steal bits of prey caught by large predators like wolves and bears. For the Haida, the raven is a wily trickster-transformer who created the world, while in Norse mythology, the ravens Hugin and Munin represented thought and memory.

Western Bluebird

Resting on a wrangler's work-worn chaps, this western bluebird (right) may be guarding a nest in a nearby yellow pine or oak, or perhaps under a loose board in the cabin. His cinnamon-chestnut breast and rusty upper mantle blend with rich blue wing and tail feathers (bottom middle), creating a brushed effect more subtle than the coloring of his more brightly clad cousins, the eastern (bottom right) and all-blue mountain (bottom left) species.

Before winter is really over, while the beaver are still snug in their lodges, the first Western bluebirds arrive on the lower slopes of the Rocky Mountains. And before long—sometimes as early as March—they have begun their courtship. Even before the pasqueflowers have appeared above the alpine snows, flashes of blue can be seen in the valleys and open wooded parts of the region—evidence that mating season has begun. The male perches beside the female, caressing her and offering her choice beetles or caterpillars. Once these gifts have been accepted, he takes her on a nest-hunting expedition, and they peer into old woodpecker holes and fencepost cavities until she finds one to her liking.

The bluebird's splendid cerulean feathers actually contain no blue pigment. They only appear to be blue because light waves of that color are reflected from a layer of cells just above the brown basal cells in their feathers' barbs.

A WENATCHEE FIELD TRIP

Barely shaded by the open stand of Ponderosa pines, I walked through the motionless air, looking for the best subject to paint. I was one of a number of artists who'd been invited to the Wenatchee River watershed near the Cascade Mountains in Washington state, an area threatened by human development including industrial logging. A conservationist group had invited us to create an exhibit that would help preserve its natural beauties. We had only one week to produce our work.

So far, nothing had caught my imagination, but the jigsawed orange-gold bark of these towering pines was beginning to suggest the patterns that signal the evolution of a new painting. As I started sketching, a flash of black and white entered the hot, dry afternoon and attached itself to a pine cone on the next tree. In a moment, the empty day had been transformed into a circus of activity as a white-headed woodpecker pried out the pine seeds and I drew rapidly, recording the way it kept its balance by holding its tail against the cone (left).

Spotted Owl

Stray beams of September sunlight filtered through the high canopy of Douglas fir, and the wind sighed as it does only in old-growth forests. We were waiting at the nest area of a spotted owl, one of the endangered birds of the Pacific Northwest. The dense old woodlands of this region are an important breeding ground for these owls because their decaying timber spawns the fungi that northern flying squirrels like to eat—and flying squirrel is one of the spotted owl's favorite meals. Unfortunately, clearcut logging has destroyed much of the bird's habitat, in spite of restrictions imposed since it was listed as an endangered species in the United States.

The owls themselves never appeared in that moss-covered forest, but as luck would have it, a tiny mountain chickadee with its distinctive white eye stripe came into view (above). On another trip to the Pacific Northwest, I did discover a young spotted owl perched on an old pine branch (right). I painted its portrait as a symbol of hope that future generations will still enjoy the presence of this reclusive species.

Robert Bateman 2001

Osprey

At a bend in the Wenatchee River, I came upon these two young osprey late one afternoon as they were mustering up the courage to leave home (left). The fledgling on the left was testing its wing strength; the one on the right was assessing the risks and benefits of leaving the safety of its branchy nest. The bird at the bottom right is their father, who was helping them make up their minds by studiously turning his back on them and refusing to bring them any fish.

Common Merganser

On a quieter part of the Wenatchee, the tossing rapids leveled out and the turquoise-green mountain water lapped softly around a sandbar. These common mergansers (above) were actually farther downstream, but I placed them in this landscape, where the triangular bank provided a stable counterpoint to the busy, curving shapes of the mergansers' bodies. The bird nearest the shore is a female, accompanying a crèche of young from a number of nests. Later, another mother will return to stand guard while this one launches into the water to dine on fingerling fish.

Dipper

When I left the osprey, I went on to look for a fast part of the river, where I could paint moving water. Like fire, rapids shift and reshape themselves in mesmerizing ways, but as I've studied these variations, I've discovered repeated patterns, determined by the forces of gravity. I showed these swirling designs in the painting above and only later added the dipper, a starling-sized bird that thrives near fast-flowing mountain streams.

Although they do not have webbed feet, dippers, like penguins, can swim underwater using their wings, and they fly through dangerous waterfalls in search of their insect larva prey. John Muir, the nineteenth-century Yosemite naturalist, called dippers the "hummingbird[s] of blooming waters" and admired their feisty cheer as they sang in winter and in summer "independent ... of sunshine and of love, requiring no other inspiration than the stream."

CANYONS AND DESERTS OF ARIZONA

Serious birders travel to southeastern Arizona to discover birds seen nowhere else north of the Mexican border. The lowlands and "sky islands," or rocky mountain outcrops, of this region cover such a range of temperature and vegetation that they provide natural lodgings for an enormous variety of creatures. One canyon in the Santa Rita Mountains, for instance, contains over one hundred bird species, including elegant trogons, painted redstarts (below), and fourteen kinds of hummingbirds. The southeast is also home to the redfaced and olive warblers, and the magnificent, blackchinned, Costa's, and broadbilled hummingbirds.

It was in southeastern Arizona that I saw my first elegant trogon. More often heard than seen, their hoarse barking sounds drift down the canyons followed by about four more downslurred notes. This time, however, I eventually found the trogon itself, perched on a live oak (left). It was as if I'd been ushered into the presence of a benign but enigmatic forest spirit. The richly colored red and green bird sat motionless, its barred tail hanging straight down like a folded shawl. It acknowledged my presence only by turning its head slowly and gazing at me with its large eyes.

Like elegant trogons, magnificent hummingbirds (above) perch and feed in deciduous woodlands along the streams and mountain slopes of southeastern Arizona and into Mexico. They are larger and move more slowly than many other hummingbirds, but against the background of the trogon's tranquility, they appear speedy and elusive as they flit and whir, hawking insects from mid-air and feeding on nectar and spiders.

Harris's Hawk

As the sun beats down on the mesquite trees and sagebrush thickets, Harris's hawks come flying low over the brushland like little squadrons of fighter planes. Named after a friend of John James Audubon, these hawks nest in social groups of up to seven birds and hunt in teams. One or two might chase a rabbit or wood rat through a thicket while the others wait on the opposite side to capture it. If their prey is already in open country, several hawks may pounce on it from different directions, giving it no hope of escape.

The group on the right is perched in a broken-down saguaro cactus, its woody skeleton exposed like the frame of a half-demolished building. At nesting time, after the female lays her eggs, other members of the colony will help incubate them and bring in food supplies.

Scrub Jay

The branches of Arizona's oak trees may also shelter pairs of Western scrub jays like the two in the painting above. They are not as community oriented as their Florida scrub jay cousins, but the parents and their offspring do stay together for a year. Western scrub jays spend the summer in canyons and river valleys, eating insects and their eggs, but in the fall, they begin hiding acorns in the ground, sometimes stealing provisions from the caches of acorn woodpeckers. Known for their intelligence and tameness toward humans, Western scrub jays can remember where they have hidden food stores after long passages of time and use special "anvil" sites to break open the hard shells of nuts.

Acorn Woodpecker

The nine-inch acorn woodpecker, seen at right, is another Arizona social nester, known for its habit of storing acorns in the custom-sized holes it bores in tree trunks and utility poles. Unlike Harris's hawks, these birds cannot live in the desert because they need to be near oak trees to harvest their food, but like the hawks, they spend their lives in communal groups. Some of these family units share storage space in a single "granary" tree, which may contain as many as fifty thousand acorns—along with some tasty insect snacks stored in the cracks and crevices of the bark.

THE GREAT PLAINS

Although I live among mountains and look out at the sea, I am always drawn to the seemingly infinite space of prairie skies and the rolling grasslands of the Great Plains. On our first autumn trip across the Prairies, Birgit and I took many detours and discovered hidden sanctuaries where bird life abounded. It was the fall migration season, and flocks of mallards and Canada geese were flying noisily overhead on their way south. At Regina, Saskatchewan, we drove northwest to Last Mountain Lake—North America's first official bird sanctuary—in hopes of seeing more migrating birds.

As we approached the north end of the lake, clumps of trembling aspen gave way to grainfields and treeless grassland. Then, beyond the reed beds at edge of the water, we saw them—wave upon wave of huge gray sandhill cranes, circling and bugling, soaring at four or five different levels and wheeling down from the stark prairie sky to land on a hilly rise in the grainfields. They'd alighted some distance away, so it was a challenge to get our bearings and head in their direction before they took off again. They moved without warning as they searched for better places to feed—fattening up on earthworms, grasshoppers, and leftover grain.

When we finally pulled up to the base of a slope where the sandhills were foraging, we trained our binoculars on the sea of gray plumage and discovered two white giants in the midst of the flock. Our hearts stopped for a moment as we realized what we had just observed. The two pale birds were whooping cranes—still rarities after coming back from the brink of extinction in the 1960s. They had attached themselves to the flock of sandhills for the journey south. We stared in awestruck silence as they fed among their companions, oblivious to our presence (opposite).

Whooping cranes in flight are sometimes confused with herons or white pelicans. Like the whoopers, white pelicans have light plumage and black wingtips, but white pelicans and herons draw their heads in toward their shoulders when they fly, while whooping cranes (like the one at left) fly with their heads and legs stretched out.

In addition to their trumpet call, sandhill cranes (below) have been known to make many unusual noises. Some have even been caught snoring while sleeping on their roosts.

Pintail

The journey to Last Mountain Lake was only one of the side trips that brought us great rewards. In fact, Birgit and I usually head off the beaten track on our birding expeditions, using detailed birdfinding guides to look for little-known nesting and feeding grounds. It takes longer to arrive at our final destination, but that is one of the beauties of birding. Looking for birds gives you a reason to slow down and enjoy the natural world.

Among the more lively places we have visited this way are the tiny prairie ponds known as potholes. Carved out by retreating glaciers at the end of the Pleistocene Age and reshaped by wallowing buffalo, they are the preferred breeding habitat for most of the mallards in North America. By mid-April, these waterbirds, along with thousands of pintails, ruddy ducks, and canvasbacks, congregate in the potholes, seeking mates and feasting on bulrush seeds and mosquito larvae (right). By May, when the blue flax and wild columbine have bloomed in prairie meadows, the down-filled nests of most mallard pairs will contain about eight eggs. A month or so later, the female will lead her stripe-faced offspring down to the water, where she will raise them with no help from the drake.

I am always struck by the quietly rich coloring and tidy markings of the northern pintail (above). The elegant male sports genteel gray, black, and white feathers, accented by a rich chocolate brown head. His more demure mate displays paler tones, but shares the same graceful profile, complete with the elongated tail feathers that give these birds their name.

Robert Bateman 2000

Western Grebe

It is the dramatic white sweep of the western grebe's throat that attracts me to this waterbird (above). Known as a "swan grebe" because of its pale coloring and softly curving neck, this marsh- or lake-dwelling bird is actually most like a loon, with its long, pointed bill and legs set far back on its body. And, like loons, grebes perform a courtship ballet in mating season. The grebe version is called "rushing."

The male begins his courtship by offering the female a mouthful of weeds, which they pass back and forth from bill to bill. But the tenderness of that interchange is abruptly broken as both grebes stand straight upright and shoot across the surface of the marsh like crazed water skiers in a kerfuffle of pattering feet.

Among the winter treats at home on Salt Spring Island is the arrival of flocks of these elegant grebes. It is their seasonal haven when the prairie potholes are frozen solid.

Redhead

Like grebes, redheads have legs set far back on their bodies—which helps them dive for roots and shoots in prairie potholes. The male redhead's markings have none of the uniformity of the grebes' deftly sweeping lines, but his massive blocks of color are equally arresting. Against the backdrop of a cool prairie dawn, his chestnut-red head and dusky-blue bill look incongruously tropical.

During the fall migration season, this pair (above) will fly toward warmer climes, congregating with other species of ducks before heading to their wintering grounds. We have seen redheads from the western Prairies on the Pacific coast, and birds from the eastern Prairies flock on Lake St. Clair and Lake Erie. There they consort with canvasbacks and scaups in rafts of as many as twenty to forty thousand before moving on to the American Atlantic coast, where they spend the winter.

Many young mallards, like the ones at right, are born near prairie potholes and raised in their waters.

Prairie Falcon

In the dead center of a hot prairie day, the air shimmers over the bleached grasses, and the wind is about as refreshing as a furnace blast. Time seems to have stopped altogether, and you would think that all birds would be snoozing somewhere under a scrap of shade. But that's when I've seen a shadow pass over the empty spaces and looked up to see the unmistakably steady wing-beat of the prairie falcon (right). The raptor was perhaps fifteen miles from its nest, hunting for a tasty ground squirrel or gray partridge. Viewed from below, its wing feathers looked like an unfurled umbrella with horizontal black stripes. From other angles, the falcon had the appearance of a pale peregrine. When the hard-working predator had caught enough for dinner, it would return to its nest—possibly on a cliff ledge above a willow-lined riverbank—where its young would feast on the catch of the day.

Burrowing Owl

In the painting below, I've shown the typically feisty appearance of the burrowing owl. This ground-dwelling bird is no pushover. When faced with an invader, it will bob up and down a few times, then attack—or dive into the abandoned gopher hole it calls home. When young burrowing owls feel threatened, they retreat to the back of their nest and make a hissing noise that sounds like a rattlesnake.

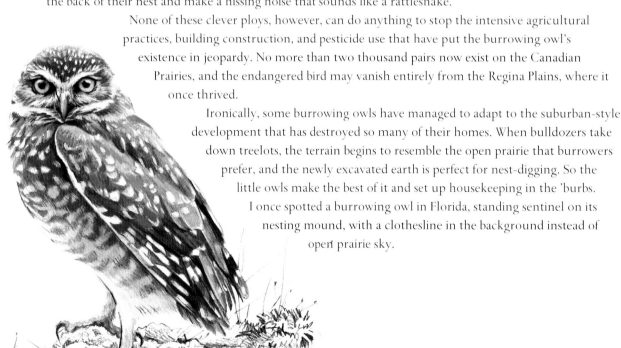

None of these clever ploys, however, can do anything to stop the intensive agricultural practices, building construction, and pesticide use that have put the burrowing owl's existence in jeopardy. No more than two thousand pairs now exist on the Canadian Prairies, and the endangered bird may vanish entirely from the Regina Plains, where it once thrived.

Ironically, some burrowing owls have managed to adapt to the suburban-style development that has destroyed so many of their homes. When bulldozers take down treelots, the terrain begins to resemble the open prairie that burrowers prefer, and the newly excavated earth is perfect for nest-digging. So the little owls make the best of it and set up housekeeping in the 'burbs.

I once spotted a burrowing owl in Florida, standing sentinel on its nesting mound, with a clothesline in the background instead of open prairie sky.

SPRING ON THE GREAT LAKES

Spring comes all at once to the beech and maple groves of southern Ontario. When I was growing up in that part of Canada, I loved every season, but I always looked forward with special delight to those first warm days of May. In Toronto, the Norway maples that lined the streets were covered with lime green flowers, and fresh new buds appeared on the branches. This simultaneity of motion and growth happens suddenly every year, when a warm front moves up the Mississippi from the Gulf of Mexico—and with that system of hot, humid air come the first waves of migrating songbirds like the rose-breasted grosbeak (above). Some warblers fly nonstop for eighty hours from their wintering grounds in South America to the Eastern Seaboard, the equivalent of a human being running four-minute miles for the same amount of time. And their timing is perfect.

The warm winds that send them north also create a paradise of growth, and the new arrivals are soon revived as they feast on birch and basswood buds and on insects rich in the proteins they need to build up their weakened bodies. The Canada warbler (below) is hunting for insects in a blossoming pear tree.

When I lived in Toronto, graceful stands of elms arched over many of the streets, and I would sometimes find the nests of Baltimore orioles swinging precariously at the ends of their branches. In the painting at left, I have shown a male Baltimore among the softly hanging leaves of a weeping willow—another good location for an oriole's home.

Robert Bateman (1980)

Scarlet Tanager, Blackburnian Warbler, Black-Throated Green Warbler

On warm May days when I lived in southern Ontario, I spent many hours in the woods, looking into the high canopies of sugar maples and oaks, where scarlet tanagers liked to hide. In spite of my searches, I heard them more often than I saw them. Their sprightly song sounded like a robin with a sore throat. The bird in the painting opposite is perched among the jewel-like catkins of a springtime aspen.

The warblers that land on the shores of Lakes Erie and Ontario go on to points north, where they nest and feed in the same spruce or pine tree as other warbler species. A Blackburnian warbler (left) might be seen on the very tip of a hemlock, its brilliant orange breast blazing in the sunlight. Farther down the tree, the black-throated green warbler (right) builds its nest and sings "*Zee zee zee zoo zee.*" Myrtle and bay-breasted warblers live at lower levels, on the bare or lichen-covered bases of the tree's branches. With this cooperative arrangement, a single tree can provide many warblers with shelter from the summer heat and plenty of buds and insects for their young.

American robins are more closely related to Eurasian blackbirds than European robins, but homesick settlers gave them the name they have today because their red breasts reminded them of the cheerful robins they had known at home. The Chippewas also associated robins with happiness, seeing them as harbingers of peace and joy. In reality, however, robins are aggressive in defending their territory, and one male will sometimes purposely collide with another in a running tackle. Robins have also been known to get drunk. A birder friend of mine once found scores of them staggering on a roadside near San Francisco. They'd been fueling up on fermented pyracantha berries during the fall migration run.

American Robin

Robins nest close to human habitations, and they are especially attracted to front porches, which provide both shelter and freedom for the parent birds (above) to fly in and out. But when I painted the Victorian verandah at left, I was using it as an innocent backdrop for a potentially threatening turn of events. Unfortunately, domestic cats also have a fondness for lounging on porches, and they are ready and waiting when the nestlings make their first attempts to fly. In fact, house cats are the worst enemy of birds in urban areas. Domestic cats kill millions of birds every year—and young robins (left) are often among their victims. Keeping housecats inside would save the lives of many songbirds.

Cliff Swallow

My childhood summers at our cottage in Ontario's Haliburton lake district were filled with the life of a bygone era. On the farm next door, hay was still brought in from the field on a horsedrawn wagon, and instead of concentrating on one species, as is so often done today, the farmer raised a mix of different animals. The barn was a sanctuary for swallows, which swooped outside in elegant ellipses before entering the silent, wood-paneled spaces where they raised their young. Barn swallows were the most common, often building their cup-like nests on beams close to the ceiling. But our neighbor's barn also sheltered cliff swallows (right), which made their homes under the outside eaves. Since these swallows were relatively rare, we felt privileged to see them every year, as they plastered mud pellets against the wall to create their gourd-shaped nests.

House Wren

The finely worked iron gate above is on one of the original Bateman farms in eastern Ontario. I like to think of my father as a boy, lifting the latch and going through to the barn. On that day, the ancestor of this little wren might have been scolding the intruder or exuberantly trilling an ode to the summer afternoon. To me, the wren's song is the free-form music of a day in the countryside, but to the bird, this ebullient performance is a normal part of his daily duties as gatekeeper to his territory.

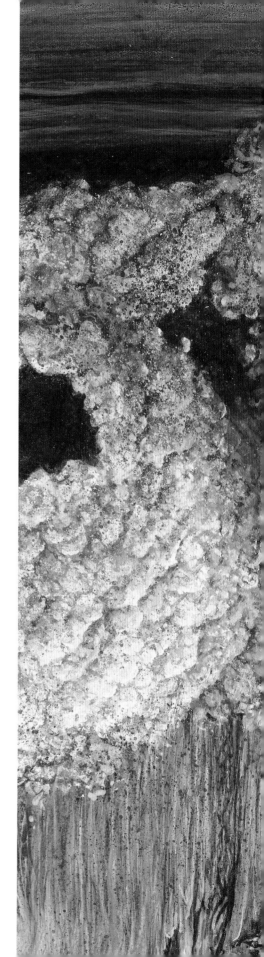

Robert Bateman 2001©

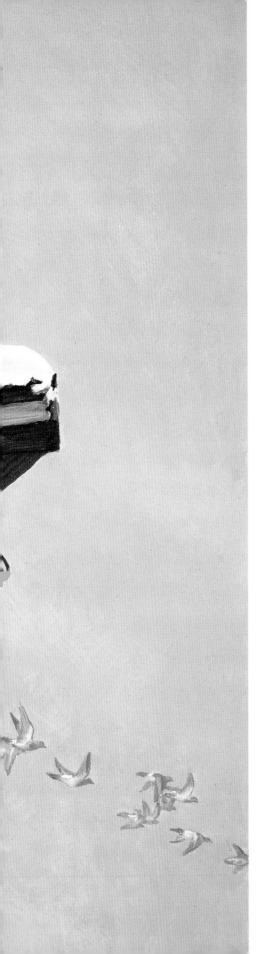

IMMIGRANTS

North America has received immigrants for hundreds of years, many of whom have had a great impact on the environment, for better and for worse. The granary on the left, for instance, was built by farmers in southern Ontario, on land where much of the old-growth forest had been permanently wiped out by their European forebearers. I particularly enjoy painting some of these remnants of our human immigrant heritage. It is a pity that the philosophy of the mid-twentieth century did not include respect for the carefully crafted structures of our ancestors. So many have been destroyed.

Starling and Rock Dove

Like their human counterparts, starlings (right, and on the chimney at left) have brought both novelty and harm to the landscapes and wildlife of this continent. These European natives were first released in New York City's Central Park in 1890 by well-meaning citizens who wanted to populate the United States with every bird mentioned in the works of Shakespeare. Although their bright yellow bills and spotted winter plumage have a lively and textured appearance, their presence has also been destructive—as the starlings have thrived by invading the homes of cavity nesters like flickers and bluebirds.

The rock doves, seen flying past the granary at left and also below left, are descendants of birds brought to Nova Scotia by the French in the early seventeenth century. Since then, they have proliferated in farm country and in cities, where they are more commonly known as pigeons. Their vast numbers have devalued them in the eyes of some, but to me, the intricate patterns and varied colors of these sometimes iridescent, sometimes pure white birds, make them interesting subjects to paint.

Robert Bateman 2001

Ring-Necked Pheasant

One midwinter day when I was in my teens, I was tramping through a favorite birding haunt—a cattail marsh north of the city. Many of the creatures in the wetland were lying low or hibernating, so my tread was not my usual stealthy one. In fact, I crashed and crunched along the icy terrain, enjoying the frozen freedom of the day.

Usually, ring-necked pheasants sit still or try to hide when they sense danger, but this time my noisy footsteps sent a male bursting skyward in a near-vertical takeoff, uttering his screeching croak as he went. Then, less than twenty-five feet above my head, a peregrine falcon dived out of nowhere. It hit the pheasant with its fist-like talons, feathers flew, and the pheasant flapped and croaked as it made a beeline for cover.

This richly colored bird (below) was perhaps too large as a peregrine target, but it was first brought to Europe and then to America as a prize for hunters and a delicacy for the table. The North American imports were brought from China in the mid-nineteenth century about the time that my ancestors were leaving Ireland and approaching the continent from the opposite direction.

The rusty voice I heard on that winter marshland day is about the best a pheasant can produce for a "song" as he stands flapping on tiptoe (left), bearing a fair resemblance to his cousin, the barnyard rooster.

EASTERN FIELDS AND FORESTS

When I was growing up, the northern boundary of Toronto was at Lawrence Avenue, which today is a mid-town street. Beyond the city line lay fertile farms surrounded by old rail fences, oak and maple woods, and meadows alive with the sounds of summer. That abounding natural world now lies silent under city streets, but before the arrival of urban sprawl, meadowlarks and bobolinks (right) sang and soared above those splendid fields, their shadows grazing the Queen Anne's lace and plush-leafed mullein plants. They have all disappeared, but their variegated melodies have stayed permanently in my memory. Whenever I recall their music, I'm taken back to those June days when the pure air was full of life and the promise of summer.

Years later on cool spring mornings northwest of the city, I would hear the songs of vesper sparrows (below) as they announced their territories in breezy, open spaces. Like many birders, I regularly participated in the "breeding bird census"—an annual ritual in which volunteers all over North America count every bird they hear or see in one spot, in the space of exactly three minutes. We went out in teams of three—one timekeeper, one recorder, and myself as observer. For the observer, hearing is the most important part of the exercise, and I identified the many vespers, still invisible in the early light, by their sweet, wild call preceded by two or three clear whistled notes.

It's an exhilarating challenge to sort through the choruses of hundreds of birds—not only vesper sparrows, but savannah sparrows, song sparrows, chipping sparrows, and a dozen other species—but it's also important work. Bird-census volunteers are preparing statistics that reveal changes in bird distribution and offer early warnings of population declines.

Turkey Vulture

In the 1960s and 1970s, when I was living in southern Ontario's Halton County, I bought a ten-acre property right next to the Niagara Escarpment, a high ridge of land extending from Niagara Falls to the Bruce Peninsula. On spring mornings, I would sometimes look up into the trees and discover feathery lumps perched at different levels among their branches. They were turkey vultures (below and right), hunched over and waiting for the sun to warm up the earth, which would, in turn, create the updrafts they needed to launch into flight. During those years, I watched an increase in the populations of these birds, which were relatively rare in my childhood. Like the cardinal and house finch, they have been gradually extending their range to the north.

Turkey vultures have never been considered beauties at close range, but in the air they hold their wings in a dihedral V that gives them a striking silhouette. They scout the landscape for food, keeping an eye on fellow vultures. Recent studies have shown that they use their remarkable sense of smell to find hidden carrion. As soon as one locates a carcass, the others coast down on their thermals and maneuver themselves toward the feast.

These birds are also well adapted to a life of scavenging. Their necks and heads are featherless, preventing the bacteria and parasites in their carrion diet from accumulating on their bodies. And high-powered enzymes and acids in their stomachs make them immune to decaying food, which would transmit botulism or other diseases to humans.

Once considered to be a bird of prey like hawks, owls, and eagles, turkey vultures have been recategorized as a result of DNA analysis and other studies—and are now thought to be more closely related to storks.

Red-Tailed Hawk

In Western movies, the hoarse, high-pitched "*kee-er-rr*" of the red-tailed hawk (above) always means something bad is about to happen, but to my mind, this bird is a sign of nothing but good. In the winter, many a bleak landscape is brought to life by the sight of this common buteo watching from its perch for some sign of a mouse, its tail feathers draped down like the skirt of a Roman centurion (left), or soaring in high circles, uttering its rasping call. Even in Toronto's rush-hour traffic, my heart has been lifted when I've seen the pirouette of a red-tail over a jammed freeway. This buteo seems to be thriving in many regions of North America, despite the pressures of human development.

American Kestrel

The American kestrel is a superbly designed, compact falcon with unusually elegant plumage. I think it looks like a tiny aristocrat, with an intricate tapestry of white, blue, and reddish feathers on its upper body and a breast decorated with dark ermine markings. The dapper kestrel is also a clever hunter. As it flies over fields, it faces into the wind for extra lift and separates the feathers at the ends of its wings to eliminate noisy turbulence on the upper surface. Then it stops and hovers while searching the ground for grasshoppers and mice. Because of this habit, the kestrel is sometimes known as a windhover, and under that name, became the "dapple-dawn-drawn falcon" of Gerard Manley Hopkins' famous "Windhover" poem.

Kestrels have excellent vision and can also see ultraviolet light. This is an advantage when they are hunting voles, whose urine reflects that part of the spectrum. And like football players who put lampblack under their eyes, the kestrel has a dark vertical line on each cheek that absorbs blinding sunlight.

Raptors, or birds of prey, use a variety of hunting methods, and their bodies are adapted to suit their individual styles. Buteos, like the red-tailed hawk, are soaring hawks which benefit from the wide surface area of their broad, rounded wings and tails to lift themselves high into the air on updrafts. Falcons have the opposite shape: their long, pointed wings and slim tails allow them to fly at high speeds and make surprise attacks on their prey. Accipiters, including goshawks (seen below), move like guided missiles through tangled woods, looping through thickets and leaning into sharp turns in pursuit of their prey. For maneuverability, they rely on their long tails; for safety, they have short, rounded wings that are not easily snared in the twisted underbrush.

Buteo   Falcon   Accipiter

©Robert Bateman—

Saw-Whet Owl

Saw-whet owls (right) are migratory and often wander south in their search for food. In my childhood birding days, they would sometimes gather during migration on the islands in Toronto's harbor—one of my favorite birding haunts. My friends and I would take the ferry to that bird haven on autumn weekends and spot the saw-whets in the dense undergrowth at the island's edge, their lemon-yellow eyes staring right back at us through a patch of wild grapes or dogwood.

At night, this little hunting bird is wary and its senses are sharp, but during the day it is one of the most lethargic of its family, making it easy prey for the much larger barred owl. Fortunately, at seven inches high, the saw-whet is also the smallest owl east of the Mississippi, so it can tuck itself into tangles or tiny cavities to escape the talons of its predatory relative.

The saw-whet does not hoot. Instead, it makes a series of low toots and a rasping noise that sounds like the filing of a saw, and that is where it gets its common name.

Eastern Screech Owl

I often made special expeditions with my boyhood birding friends to see screech owls in the old orchards just north of Toronto. There were plenty of nesting places there, in hollows where limbs had broken away from the trunks of the older trees. Our greatest hope was to spot one nestled in a cavity, looking as if it was surveying the neighborhood from its front porch. To bring the birds out of their hiding places, we would sometimes make a K-note call, kissing the backs of our knuckles and making a sound like a rodent in distress. (This is the best way to attract an owl or a fox.) Sometimes we'd look for a cavity where we'd noticed an owl before and were surprised to find the bird gone. But on our way out of the orchard, we would try again and discover an adult owl had been sitting there the whole time, concealing the hole and looking exactly like a piece of bark (right).

Screech owls are dimorphic—that is, they come in two colors, red and gray. Until partway through the nineteenth century, naturalists thought the red "phases" were females or young, but eventually they realized that the colors were not dependent on sex or age. The owls' name is open to some misinterpretation as well: screech owls don't actually screech; they make a mournful, quavering sound, which has earned them the more appropriate label of "shivering owl" in the American South.

Robert Bateman 2001

Great Horned Owl

I couldn't believe my ears. A great horned owl was hooting outside our window in the middle of the day. This giant of the dark forests had been a mystical bird for me for as long as I could remember, and during my youth, I'd spent many hours searching the wooded areas near Toronto for signs of this owl—usually pellets of rodent bones wrapped in fur, which the birds regurgitate after their meals. I would scrutinize the gloomy pines overhead, but if the owl was there, it would be almost impossible to see. Sometimes the presence of a great horned would be betrayed by a flock of clamoring, mobbing crows. Then my best view of the bird would be a gray-brown shape fleeing to a more secure hiding place in the depths of the woods.

After moving to our home near the Niagara Escarpment, I had occasionally been treated to the sonorous night-time notes of the male or the higher tones of the female. But now I was looking straight at a male giving his courtship call from a beech tree less than a hundred feet from our dining-room window (right). The ear tufts, or horns, were laid back, and with each hoot, the majestic bird would hunch forward and inflate his throat feathers. I had never seen this performance before and have not seen it since. It was one of the privileged moments birders always seek.

Great horned owls are found in suitable habitat all over North America. Their plumage differs greatly, however, from dark blackish brown to an extremely pale mottled gray in the frosty north. On one visit to a rehabilitation center, I was so enchanted by a pale-headed great horned owl named Samantha (below) that I painted her portrait on the spot.

"Samantha"

Robert Bateman
Sept 17/2000.

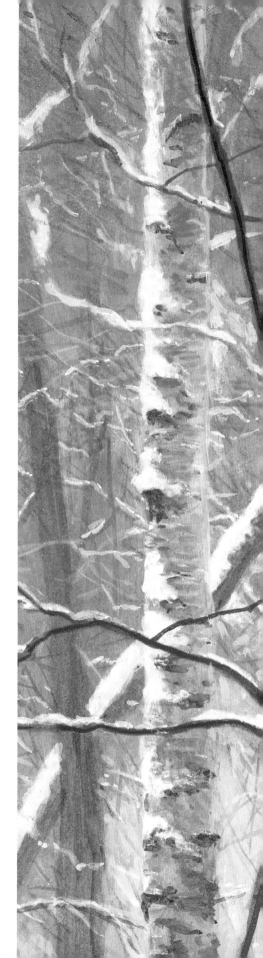

Hairy and Downy Woodpeckers

In the muffled silence of the winter woods, warmth and life may seem completely buried under the blanketing snow. Then the cheerful percussion of a tapping woodpecker will break the silence and its red and black-speckled markings will appear on the side of a pine or birch. Sometimes the bird pecking away at the bark is a downy woodpecker (above); sometimes it's the slightly larger and longer-billed hairy woodpecker (right). The two species look so similar that I cannot count all the times I've seen one or the other and asked myself, "Is it a hairy or a downy?" When people start asking questions like this, they are beginning to see the world as a birder sees it. This way of observing the environment began for me at about the age of twelve—the year I started my first bird list. Out in the field, surrounded by a rich world of trees, shadows, and varied plumage, more questions present themselves: Does the bird seem to have a heavy-ish bill or a petite one? Is its body about nine inches or closer to six inches long? After some experience, the questions are not always so specific. You just get the feel of the distinctions between similar species.

Hairy and downy woodpeckers can be identified mostly by size. The hairy has a larger body and a larger bill, and its sharp call also sounds "bigger." But getting a glimpse of some actual plumage is, of course, a great advantage. The hairy's outer tail feathers are clear and white, while those of the downy have a few black marks. For birders, these are important details—and there are great rewards in paying attention to them, as naming creatures gives people a sense of understanding and participating in the natural world.

Pileated Woodpecker

Pileated woodpeckers are by far the most spectacular North American woodpeckers, but they are much more common than most people might imagine. This pair is whacking holes in an old pine trunk, digging for hibernating insects. But they can often be seen flying across a road or through a woodlot. From a distance, they can easily be mistaken for crows until you notice their bounding flight—and, if you are lucky, catch sight of their red crests. If you are listening for the sound, you can also detect their presence by their ringing calls or by their loud drumming as they search for insects and build nests in trees.

In spring, both the male and the female do the nest-building work, drilling with such force that their bills hit the tree at about twenty-five miles an hour. Even though they take turns, that impact could explode their mandibles and knock them unconscious if they did not have special adaptations. Their strong skulls and bill muscles act as shock absorbers; their brains are surrounded by tough outer membranes; and their jaws are held together by a special locking mechanism.

ON INLAND WATERS

Beyond the bustle of urban Ontario, the countryside is home to thousands of secret sanctuaries—ponds, lakes, and marshes—where Canada geese feed on the waterside grasses and herons stand like sculptures, waiting for fish to come within striking range. I have spent many hours on the banks and shores of these inland waters, interpreting the shifting water patterns, the curve of a wing, or the shadow of snow cast over a stream.

One winter day I observed the pair of Canada geese at right as they lifted off—heading, perhaps, for a grainfield where they could forage on gleanings from the autumn harvest. The velvet-black necks and panda-white cheek patches of these birds were not part of the winter landscape when I was growing up in Ontario because they always migrated south. But warming climate trends have encouraged many to spend the winter in temperate zones, where grass and grain are no longer covered by snow for the entire season. In parks and playing fields, Canada geese can become an overbearing presence as they lunch on grass at rates of up to seventy blades a minute.

Red-Winged Blackbird

When I was a teenager, male red-winged blackbirds would begin to reappear in marshes and roadside ditches in February and March as southern Ontario emerged from the frozen winter. It was always a landmark event to hear the first red-wing of the season, since they were relatively uncommon at that time and their call was a sure sign of spring. They would arrive in the wetlands when snow was still clustered around the clumps of tousled cattails and cling to bulrush stalks in the wind-whipped cold, their flashy red and yellow shoulder patches hidden under their black body feathers.

Then, as the weather warmed and the ice began to melt, the marsh would become busy with red-wings perched higher up on the stems, fluffing out their feathers and piercing the air with their unmistakable "*Ogalee-geeee! Ogalee-geeee!*" (left). Later, they would sing around the borders of their territory to establish dominance, aggressively displaying their red and yellow shoulder patches.

At nesting time, each speckly brown-striped female (above) builds her own nest of cattails and sedges, lashing it to a swaying stalk with plant stems. The polygamous male gives her no help at all in brooding or feeding, but noisily defends the homes of his several mates. If a hawk or crow dares to approach, the red-wing lunges at it, often with the help of other males in the marsh.

Since my earliest birding days, the red-wings have undergone a population explosion. Large-scale agriculture has created vast, open fields, where they feed on crops, including grain spilled from mechanical harvesters. In the fall, a troupe of ten thousand might also descend on a cornfield, stripping the husks down a bit and nibbling a row or so off every cob. Birders are beginning to notice more and more red-wings wintering over next to these abundant supplies of food.

Great Blue Heron

All was quiet in the wetland except for the sounds of frogs jumping and ducks flapping and quacking in the late afternoon sun. As I sat at the edge of the marsh, studying the water's changing patterns and colors, the surface appeared to be motionless but it was actually shifting constantly as the sky became cloudy or bright or the wind changed direction. I imagined myself in the intimate world of the great blue heron, where shadows and surface ripples can mean a meal or where a moving branch or snapping twig can signal the arrival of a dangerous intruder. But the greatest dangers cannot be detected by the elegant, sharp-eyed heron (right and below). Industrial chemicals in the food chain, wetland drainage, tree cutting, and housing developments are destroying rookeries that may have existed for centuries.

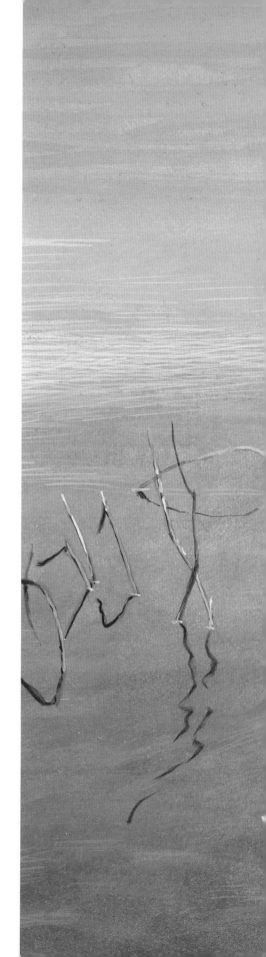

Common Loon

Since my childhood summers at our cottage in Haliburton, the loon has come to symbolize, for me and many others, the magic of the north. As a very young boy, I thought the first part of the bird's eerie call sounded a bit like a wolf's cry, but the final "laughter" gave away the fact that I was hearing the great diver of the boreal lakes. In those days there were no motorboats on the lake and the loons lived a carefree but secretive existence.

Over the years, I continued to be drawn to the loon's prehistoric cry, but the precious triumph of finding its nest had always eluded me, no matter how quietly I paddled into sheltered coves. When I finally discovered one, it literally came to me in a flash—a flash of bubbles and wings grazing past me while I was snorkeling in the shallow waters beside a granite island. Since I'd been absorbed with minnow watching, I hadn't noticed the mother loon, who'd become alarmed at the sight of this weird, besnorkeled water creature. I was only a foot or so from shore, and when I surfaced, two beautiful olive-colored eggs came into view just inches above water level, set on a wet, grassy nest. I returned to that granite island in the fall and painted the flotilla of loons at left congregating before their southward migration.

THE ATLANTIC COAST

As we approached the edge of the cliff, we passed through a wind-blown world of grassy hummocks and ancient rock. Between us and the crashing ocean stood dozens of diminutive, chalk-faced puffins—part of a colony of 160,000 pairs who spend the breeding season on Great Island, off Newfoundland's southeastern shore.

Other puffins were flying in or out of their nesting burrows, hurtling through the air like stub-winged bumblebees.

But the puffins were not alone. Herring gulls twice the size of the foot-high birds had set up territories in and around the colony, standing at its edges like sentinels on the walls of a fort while kittiwakes lined the ledges beneath (left). The gulls' choice of location was no accident. They had positioned themselves next to the puffins' grassy burrows so they would never be far from dinner— and they'd learned to let puffins do most of their food-gathering work.

Like other members of the Auk family, puffins are terrible aviators, but they fly long distances to fish for capelin and sand launce to feed themselves and their chicks. They kill their prey with the sharp tips of their bills, then flip it to the backs of their mouths and hold it there with their spiny tongues. This efficient system allows them to carry at least two fish at a time—and sometimes as many as thirty. With their catch held fast in their beaks, the birds then begin the long journey home, where they will feed their young. But before any puffin reaches its burrow, the bird is often greeted by a bullying gull. This superb flier dives and pecks at the puffin until it drops the fish—which the gull then snatches in mid-air (right).

After this unpleasant encounter, the puffin has no choice but to fly all the way back to the fishing grounds, leaving its hungry chick in the burrow and the gull standing at the front entrance. Eventually, the young puffin becomes so famished that it tries to leave its nest. This is exactly what the gull has been waiting for. As soon as the chick comes close enough, the predator grabs it and gobbles it up.

Robert Bateman 2002

Northern Gannet

Although most gannet colonies are massive communities at the tops of sea cliffs, these seabirds may also be seen perching on half-foot-wide ledges, performing pair-bonding rituals. They point their bills toward the sky and clatter them together like two sabers, flapping their wings at the same time (left). Sometimes they bow so deeply that they fall off the edge of the cliff.

Seabirds cluster around the shores of all the Atlantic provinces, but one of my favorite seabird havens is Bonaventure Island—a whale-shaped rock that rises more than two hundred feet above the Gulf of St. Lawrence, just east of Quebec's Gaspé Peninsula. From a distance, the thousands of gannets that nest there look like bands of melting snow. But they are actually about the size of geese. I am especially intrigued by their intricate faces. Their beaks are edged with lines as if someone had drawn them in with dark pencil, and their heads look as if they'd been dipped in saffron-yellow pollen.

Gannet colonies are so closely packed that when a gannet returns to her nest from a fishing expedition, she must circle like a pilot landing at an airport—avoiding the pecking beaks of her neighbors. Keeping her wings level, with her eyes fixed on the tiny landing pad, she arches her body down until her spread-out tail is completely vertical and can act as a brake. The slowdown makes her wings stall, so she can no longer stay aloft. With a deft flick, she rotates her wings upward, turning them into sails, the black pinions splayed like fans above her head. Then, with a few strong flaps of the wrist and wingtips, she stops dead and plummets straight down to the nest (above).

Robert Bateman 2002 ©

IN THE EVERGLADES

A brilliant Easter morning sun infused the sky with subtropical light as we headed down the boardwalk with our youngest sons, Christopher and Robbie. We were looking for herons and egrets, wending our way along a wooden path through the long sloping wetland known as the Florida Everglades. We were in a mangrove swamp at the edge of the water and took turns looking through the binoculars, searching for splashes of white or blue feathers among the tangled prop roots of the mangrove trees.

As the sun moved higher, we were delighted by a glimpse of pale pink feathers showing through the dark green leaves. They belonged to a group of roseate spoonbills, swinging their heads through the water to siphon off shrimps and crabs.

Likely the prettiest and most colorful plumage to be found on the mangrove swamp, the spoonbills' pink or rose feathers end abruptly at the beginning of a completely incongruous head. It is bare, like a vulture's, and features a googly eye, a wrinkly face, and a long rounded bill (left).

Unlike flamingos, which feast on algae in the salt lakes of Florida's open inland country, spoonbills enjoy the crustaceans of the sheltered mangrove shores. Eating is no simple act, however—in fact, it's almost a gymnastic feat. The bird's head swings in long arcs from side to side through the swamp water. Then its bill, held nearly vertical and open just slightly, closes in on anything it senses through the vibration detectors on the inside of the spoon.

Another bird with a uniquely adapted bill, the black skimmer (above) feeds at twilight, launching out from land in a graceful procession against the waning sun. These persistent fishing birds breed on parts of all the American coasts and south to South America, but I remember them most vividly as silent, speedy flotillas, moving along beside us as we boated through the waters of Florida.

When the black skimmer feeds, it leans into the surface of the water, then drops its two-toned bill—the longer lower mandible slicing through the water a quarter-inch below the surface. Meanwhile, the higher mandible sticks up in the air, poised to clamp down on a shrimp or minnow. The skimmer makes a first pass through the water, then switches back and propels itself along the same route, cutting through the water like scissors through fabric.

Brown Pelican

If the fishing tools of spoonbills and skimmers look like kitchen utensils, the bills of brown pelicans resemble large suitcases. But the most remarkable thing about a pelican is its size. Adults weigh in at about nine pounds and have wingspans of approximately six and a half feet—similar to a bald eagle's. Their squat and waddly bodies make them look like poor contenders for flying prizes, but contrary to all appearances, brown pelicans (right) are superb aviators. Like World War I pilots, they are saddled with equipment that looks far from airworthy, but they fly with utter grace, using the tiny air currents that bounce up off the ocean's waves to stay aloft. I've seen them sailing out beyond the shores of Florida, conforming perfectly to the water's surface without moving their wings.

When fishing for minnows or mullet, the stocky pelican first climbs to a height of about twenty-five to thirty feet, then does a quick flip and nosedives toward the water. At this point, the bird appears to be in imminent danger of a catastrophic bellyflop, but just in time, it tilts its upended rump slightly forward so the top of its bill slides through the water's surface, absorbing most of the shock of impact.

I watched this pelican in the Florida Keys (above) waterproof himself by squeezing oil out of a preen gland at the base of his tail, then combing it through his feathers.

Robert Bateman 2002

Great Egret

Great, or American, egrets are large members of the heron family with pure white feathers at all times of year. They are graceful in flight, and during breeding season both sexes grow exquisite, four-foot lacy capes, or nuptial feathers, which drape like gossamer from their backs. They roost in mangrove branches and spend much of their time squabbling over perching positions. Flapping their wings in shows of aggression, they try to intrude on each other's territory like the two on the right. I have painted them as if they were woven into the mangrove tree like escutcheons in a medieval tapestry.

Cattle Egret

North American great egrets move as far north as Massachusetts in the summer, but that pilgrimage is minor compared to the voyages of their half-sized cousins, the cattle egrets (above). In the mid- to late-nineteenth century, these birds spread from the west coast of Africa to South America—perhaps as stowaways on boats—eventually making their way north to Florida and Texas. Their habit of catching insects stirred up by the hooves of Cape buffalo and other large mammals was easily transferred to the pastures of North America, where they now follow herds of domestic cattle to feed on grasshoppers and flies. They prefer herds that move at about five to fifteen steps per minute. Faster animals force them to use too much energy to keep up; slower ones likely provide too little food. Native to Asia as well as Africa, cattle egrets can now be found even in Canada and on continents as far-flung as Australia, where they congregate with kangaroos.

Robert Bateman 2001

THE TROPICAL AMERICAS

Time and space seemed to merge into one as our thatch-roofed raft nosed out into the main current of the Madre de Dios River in southeastern Peru. The tallest trees of the rainforest stood silhouetted against the sunrise like black filigree, and mist rose from the waters of this Amazon tributary. We were headed for the clay licks, or *collpas*, on the western bank, hoping to see crowds of parrots and scarlet macaws congregating for an exotic, muddy feast. The best theory to account for the birds' habit of eating soil seems to be that some claybanks contain minerals which serve as antidotes to the poisons in the unripe fruit they eat. They harvest "green" fruit in order to compete successfully with monkeys and other upper-canopy creatures that postpone their feasts until the fruit is riper. But the trees where they feed use "chemical warfare" to deter pillagers of fruit whose seeds are not yet ready to be dispersed. Other animals might find clay unpalatable, but like all birds, scarlet macaws have little sense of taste—and unlike some, they have incredibly tough digestive systems.

Suddenly, the mist-filled world was flooded with light, and splashes of green, blue, and reddish-yellow shot through the air in front of us. Like lavish rainbows, a flock of blue-headed and orange-cheeked parrots attached themselves to the claybank and started to eat (opposite). The scarlet macaws never did leave their perches in the trees but continued to clamber through the vines and branches, using their feet like hands and their beaks like feet with the skill of gymnasts. They serenaded us with screeches, gurgles, and purrs while we watched their relatives dig into the bank, jostling each other for position.

Collared aracaris, smaller members of the Toucan family, have complex, jagged markings compared to the clean pastels of their keel-billed relatives— but their habits are similar. All toucans roost together in tree cavities and each flock has several "apartments" where the adults find shelter. To save space in these confined quarters, they hold their tails over their backs.

Like scarlet macaws, toucans weave their way through the high canopy of the rainforest, feeding on the fruit that grows in those sunny upper spaces. The keel-billed toucan I've sketched here is native to Costa Rica and Belize and is famous for its cartoon-style bill, which takes up a third of the length of the bird's twenty-inch body. This anatomical feature is not only decorative, however. It is so long that the bird can use it to pick fruit from distant branches without leaving the safety of a stable perch.

Macaws are endangered, their numbers declining because of logging and slash-and-burn farming in their rainforest habitats. Their American range, which once stretched from Mexico to Peru, is now limited to several isolated populations within that area, and the macaws that have survived reproduce very slowly, raising only one or two young every two years. To make matters worse, poachers with few other sources of income steal nestlings to be sold at high prices in the illicit bird trade. But there is some good news. Since the thieves have excellent knowledge of nesting sites and macaw behavior, conservation groups have begun to hire them as guardians and as guides for birding tours. The presence of ecotourists discourages further poaching, and the reformed poachers benefit from a legitimate income.

Robert Bateman 2002

THE GALÁPAGOS

It was still dark when we heard the anchor chain roll down. We'd spent part of the night moving from one island to the next in the Galápagos, the scattered archipelago that helped inspire Charles Darwin to develop his theory of evolution. As we moved toward the shore in our landing craft, the dawn light washed over a scene from Hades—the contorted shapes of spiny marine iguanas clinging to barren lava rocks. But this inhospitable introduction was deceiving. The Galápagos are so isolated that its birds and other animals have had little contact with humans and are therefore nearly as tame as if they lived in Eden. And they were so oblivious to us that when we walked on the designated trails, we had to be careful where we stepped because the birds didn't move away.

We moved gingerly through the close-packed colony of blue-footed boobies nesting on the ground in front of us and watched them strut around like gentlemen in spats on London's Strand. The flash-footed booby gets its name from the Spanish *bobo*, which means "clown" or "dunce." This is hardly a fair description of the birds' flying and fishing skills, but the label was likely used to describe their slapstick courting ritual, in which the male and female do a slow dance around each other, lifting their blue feet as if they were skin-diving flippers. It may also have applied to their tame and friendly nature, which made it easy for early sailors to trap them and turn them into stew.

Boobies are members of the gannet family and like their relatives, they plunge feed, sometimes *en masse*, into a school of fish. They descend like vertical bullets with their wings closed.

By ten in the morning, the heat burned around us and the light was too harsh for photography. So we abandoned birding for the day and went swimming in the cold ocean, snorkeling in the company of tame fur seals. The sky above us was a heavy blue, punctuated from time to time by the sight of angular frigatebirds with enormous red pouches cruising the skies (above and right). Like boobies, magnificent frigatebirds dive from great heights, but they are at a disadvantage in the fishing enterprise because their seven- to eight-foot wings are easily waterlogged and their legs are weak, making takeoff from the ocean next to impossible. So these plunderers, named after the pirates who once operated fast frigates, use their deeply forked tails to steer toward other fishing birds. Then they dive and harass them until they drop their prey. The sea pirate then swoops down and catches the fish before it hits the water.

Robert Bateman

Yellow-Crowned
Night Heron

Although most wild creatures on the Galápagos are exceptionally approachable, the yellow-crowned night heron is a cautious nester, brooding in groups or colonies, sometimes twenty feet up on the larger limbs of mangroves. I discovered these two (left) at the water's edge, within reach of the surging waves, hunting for the ever-present Sally Lightfoot crabs, which glow like embers in the creviced lava rocks. It was daylight, which may seem a surprising time for a night heron to be feeding, but unlike its black-crowned relative, it sometimes feeds when the sun is high. In this painting, I have tried to show the intricacy of the bird's gray-blue, almost lavender, wing. Its multiple planes consist of primaries, the long feathers at the ends of its wings that create forward propulsion during flight, and secondaries, the shorter plumes growing from the rest of the wings, which generate the lift needed to get the bird off the ground. These feathers and the ones covering the rest of the heron's body meet and overlap each other, like a many-layered scalloped curtain.

Red- and Blue-Footed Boobies

Red-footed boobies (above) are extremely difficult to spot. Unlike their beach-dwelling blue-footed cousins, they nest prudently away from the shore, making cozy abodes in the crotches of trees or perching with their feet grasping the branches like wraparound rubber.

Male blue-footed boobies (right) seem to love showing off their footwear at any time, not just during mating season. While the female is sitting on the nest, her partner may goose-step around her for a while, then take off into the air, brandishing his cool-blue feet as he goes.

Robert Bate

OLD WORLDS

The towns and countryside of Europe remind me of a tapestry, where the lives of birds and other wildlife are woven easily into everyday human activities. Throughout the Continent and the United Kingdom, cottages and cathedrals that have remained standing for hundreds of years are as permanent as hillsides or ancient trees, and the same birds return to them year after year to nest and raise their young. Such sights have always given me hope that humans can learn how to live in harmony with nature, even in places that have been densely populated for a long time.

When I first traveled to Europe in the 1950s with my friend Erik Thorn, we would spend as much time in the countryside as in the cities. After a day of visiting museums, we would leave town before dusk and head out to camp in the countryside, where we fell asleep to the sounds of robins and finches singing their evening songs. It was a perfect blending of the past and the present, of human artistry and natural wonders.

We came upon the ruin of a twelfth-century Christian church in the Connemara district of Ireland one misty autumn day (left). The old stone building was at the end of a winding woodland path on a little island in a wild lake. It seemed appropriate to add the barn owl to this setting. Its pale, soulful face and soundless flight harmonized with the ruins and the otherworldly atmosphere.

Every spring, northern Europeans greet the return of the bullfinch (above) with a mixture of pleasure and exasperation. Its rose-red breast, glossy black cap, and black tail and wings are a welcome respite as the gray days of winter come to an end. But such glamorous plumage does not compensate for the bird's habit of devouring the buds on fruit trees. One bullfinch can eat up to half the buds of a pear tree in one day—a rate of ten to thirty per minute.

122

Great Tit, Blue Tit, Blackbird, and Robin

Many years after my first discovery of Europe, our family spent an entire year living in a two-century-old farmhouse in Bavaria. The bullfinch on the previous page often appeared in the tree outside our kitchen window, and I painted him feeding on its late-summer crop of berries. Our garden was also filled with the choruses of birds that grace gardens in most parts of the Continent and the United Kingdom—Eurasian blackbirds, great tits and blue tits, and European robins. In our village—as in many others in Europe—these creatures were part of a treasured and respected natural world.

The blue tits and great tit (seen at far left) on the tree to the left are members of the same family as chickadees, and like those North American birds, they are expert gymnasts, clinging to branches and often hanging upside down to dig for insects and larvae under bark. When feeding in hedgerows with other species, a blue or great tit may spot a predator and call out a soft alarm—a signal for all the hedgerow birds to stay hidden and quiet among the branches. Each species has its own warning call, but every voice is understood by all—a universal code language designed for mutual protection.

In or near the hedgerow, you might find thrushes like the Eurasian blackbird (top right) and the European robin. Though European and American robins are members of the same thrush family, the American species is actually a closer relative of the blackbird because it is also in the same genus (a sub-group of the family).

All their lives robins sing complex but melodious songs that have the same structure as human musical compositions—each musical grouping consisting of four different motifs. I have shown the robin below played out after many summers of weaving its music through the air of woods and gardens. But this bird's offspring will carry on the musical tradition and, like its parent, may be seen foraging for grubs and worms on sunlit lawns or perching on the handles of spades left standing in worked-up gardens.

Robert Bateman. 1996©

Avocet

Avocets like the one shown above forage with their upturned bills in the Camargue wetlands at the mouth of the Rhône River, near the city of Arles. They share their Mediterranean feeding grounds with ibises, egrets, pink flamingos, and the famous wild horses of the Camargue, which were favored by Julius Caesar.

House Martin

On a day when the wide-open skies of Provence looked down on sun-baked olive groves and fields of lavender, I discovered these house martins flying in front of the cathedral at Arles (left). Only when one of them flitted under the overhang did I notice that they had sculpted their mud nests right next to the sconces and gargoyles above the cathedral's arch. In many European towns and even some cities, wild birds have lived near humans for so long that the two species co-exist amicably. The direct ancestors of these two white-rumped martins may well have built nests near the same cathedral in the days when van Gogh was painting in Provence.

Red Crossbill

I have been privileged, every so often, to be part of a group of artists invited to paint landscapes of particular ecological significance. This time, I was with the Artists for Nature Foundation in the Spanish Pyrénées, setting out every morning from our stone lodge in the mountains, looking for subjects to paint. I hiked into the open air with my easels and oils strapped to my back and worked in the field, surrounded by the sounds of birds and rushing mountain streams. After a hard day's work, I would come back with my art under my arm to compare notes with my colleagues over a wholesome meal and a glass of wine.

The birds of those mountainscapes are quite different from the ones found at lower European altitudes—and some were already familiar to me. The "*Chit-chit-chit*" of red crossbills (left) echoed sounds from an identical species, which I've heard on my mountain walks on Salt Spring Island. Found in coniferous forests on three continents—Europe, Asia, and North America—red crossbills are finches with thick, sturdy mandibles that cross over each other at the tip—a design that helps them pry seeds from spruce and pine cones.

In the painting at left, I've shown a male and female crossbill feeding on a mountain conifer. The female is pushing her beak into the cone and in a moment will lift the scale that covers the seed by moving her jaw from side to side. Then she'll snag the seed with her tongue, and grasp her apéritif.

Alpine Chough

On rocky outcrops near the high meadows of the Pyrénées, I've seen chunky black birds that look like crows at first glance (above left)—but their flight is swooping, like a swallow's. These alpine choughs are members of the crow family, though they look more like costumed acrobats with their glossy purple-black feathers and bright yellow feet and bills.

Dipper

The crystal-clear streams of Europe's mountains shelter one of the continent's most elusive birds—the dipper (above right), a white-bibbed version of the drabber brown-gray North American species. On our alpine birding trips, Birgit usually wants to catch sight of these birds before anyone else, since they are among her favorites. But they are difficult to see on rocky stream banks and even more obscure as they fly straight through waterfalls.

Capercaillie

To say that I was exhilarated would be an understatement. We were bumping along an Austrian alpine trail in a little four-wheel drive with Fritz, our guide, at the wheel. It was the late-winter mating season of the capercaillie and Fritz had guaranteed that I would see one. I was thrilled because ever since my first trip to Scotland in the 1950s, the capercaillie had been my main jinx bird. (A jinx bird is one you've wanted to see for years but for some reason you've never been at the right place at the right time and the bird has always escaped your sights.)

High in the snow-laden conifer forest, Fritz stopped the vehicle and we all got out to walk the slippery trail to the capercaillie's territory. Fritz was carrying a long broomstick, which I noticed was full of notches that had me puzzled until he explained what they were—chunks the capercaillie had taken out of the wood on a previous visit. Since it was mating season, Fritz explained, the ten-pound male grouse was aggressively defending his territory. Anyone who dared set foot in his domain could be severely injured—one photographer had been pecked so badly he'd needed hospitalization after trying to take an eye-level shot of the bird. But Fritz always went prepared and used the stick to protect himself from any attack.

As we entered the snowy grove, we could hear a rustling sound in the bushes. Then, all at once, the oversized grouse came strutting out of the dense forest into the little clearing and went for us in no uncertain terms. He snapped his formidable yellow bill and fanned out his black-tipped tail in a peacock-like display. Then he puffed out his throat feathers and began stomping around in his own version of a highland fling. I persisted in sketching the hefty dancer while Fritz brandished the broomstick. Since the encounter was even more stressful for the bird than for us, I worked as quickly as I could, and before long we were all heading back to the four-wheel drive.

Still in a state of euphoria that I had actually seen this "jinx bird" and drawn the magnificent animal in its mountain home, I rushed back down the ice-domed trail, slipped, and tore all the ligaments in one knee. The effect was indirect, but the conquering capercaillie had claimed another victim!

European Kingfisher

Several more jinx birds had been eluding me for years—including the European kingfisher, the black woodpecker, and the lammergeier vulture. Unlike North America's raucous belted kingfisher, the European species (above) is a finely worked jewel, but it is not a rare bird by any means. It just never appeared when I was in the vicinity. Finally, one evening in Spain, I stopped by a bridge and saw one fly out of a riverside glade—but only after my birding companions had seen it first!

Black Woodpecker

The black woodpecker (right) was my next challenge. After the kingfisher sighting, Birgit and I went on to the Spanish Pyrénées and spent a wonderful day hiking through the forests, climbing through snowfields, and scanning sunlit mountain peaks. But we saw nothing of the woodpecker, apart from its nest. Many years later, one finally appeared early one morning in the mountains of Spain, inspiring this painting of the purposeful jet-black bird in its favorite tree, an aspen.

Robert Bateman
2001 ©

Lammergeier Vulture

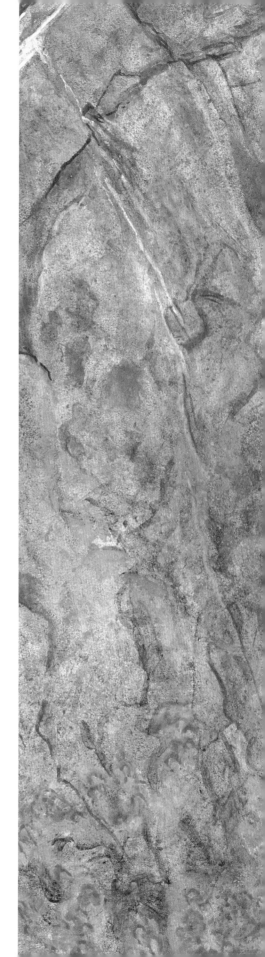

We traversed the pine-clad slope of a valley in the Spanish Pyrénées and emerged into a world of sheer rock. Directly across from us, there was a buff and slate-blue cliff where, we'd been told, a lammergeier had built its nest. We managed to spot the nest on a sheltered ledge, along with what appeared to be a half-grown chick trying its wings. Then, as the late-morning sun moved toward the top of the sky, a shadow fell across the cliffs in the near distance and darted up the mountain ridges. The falcon-like silhouette soared in slow motion, then disappeared. Finally it returned, accompanied by a second, similar shape. At last, one of the birds landed and began feeding its young—its golden neck ruff glowing regally in the sun (below). It was my first lammergeier and, strangely, I'd sighted it just a few hours after the black woodpecker. Time seems to blend with eternity at moments like this, and the flights of those dignified birds etched themselves permanently in my memory. Many months later, those opalescent images returned as I painted my memories of that magical morning (right).

The diet of lammergeiers consists mostly of the marrow of bones left behind on the feeding grounds of other scavengers. These birds are not strong enough to pry open a bone with their bills, so they pick it up in their claws and drop it on a hard surface from a height of up to two hundred feet. When the bone finally cracks open, exposing the marrow, the vulture gobbles it down whole. Bones as large as four inches in diameter can be dissolved by the bird's powerful digestive system.

Robert Bateman
2005 ©

Mute Swan

I discovered this aristocratic group of mute swans (right) in Scotland, preening and resting on a seashore dotted with sea pinks. Members of this regal family have thrived for about a thousand years in western Europe because of the many lowland millponds and streams that have provided them with food and places to build their enormous reedy nests. In past centuries, swans were so abundant in Britain and on the Continent that they were hunted or kept in "swanneries" as prize game.

Mute swans (bottom right) can be distinguished from their relatives by the elegant S-curve of their necks and the way they point their bills downward when they swim. Unlike other swans, they have no voice, apart from occasional hisses and puppy-like barks. This is because their trachea is almost straight, while those of the fully voiced trumpeter (bottom left) and tundra (bottom middle) have many bends, which act like the curves in a French horn.

Mute swans are permanent, and often quite tame, residents of western Europe, where they are joined by migrant whooper and tundra swans in winter.

In Hans Christian Andersen's tale "The Wild Swans," a wicked stepmother turns eleven princes into wild swans, and they are trapped in that state until their sister frees them. Other legends and tales have also associated swans with distress and Romantic longing. Aristotle claimed that swans really did sing a "swan song" at the approach of death and that mariners had heard whole flocks of them off the coast of Libya singing mournfully and expiring on the ocean's waters. A mortally wounded tundra, or whistling, swan is also said to utter a dying call as it tries to rejoin its flying companions.

AT THE TAJ MAHAL

At first light, the Taj Mahal does not appear to be white. Its marble facings, which are actually composed of a range of colors, from white to cream to light yellow, reflect varying shades of rose and pink. Birgit and I were standing on the lawns of the great monument one morning, studying the architecture and watching these colors change as the sun came up. Coppersmith barbets were hammering out their metallic calls, flamboyant hoopoes (below) were poking for worms in the grass with their long, curving bills, and rose-ringed parakeets flew past the domes, disappearing then reinserting themselves into the visual frame that became the painting to the left.

As we scanned the structure, we were surprised and delighted to see two dark forms perched on the ledge of a minaret. They were laggar falcons (above), preying on the pigeons which abound in the vicinity of the Taj. A bird of prey, especially a falcon, always adds distinction to a moment in nature. It was truly gilding the lily to have the sunrise, the Taj Mahal, and these falcons coming together on that golden morning.

Black Kite, Rose-Ringed Parakeet, and Red-Wattled Lapwing

Some of my most memorable Indian birding expeditions have taken place in Rajasthan—the northern state where the maharajas once ruled. The Aravalli Hills divide this former "Abode of Kings" into two territories: a desert-like region in the northwest and fertile forests and wetlands in the southeast. In those uplands, on Lake Pichola, lies Udaipur, a sixteenth-century royal city where peacocks and rose-ringed parakeets decorate the gardens and black kites perch near temples to steal food offered to the gods. We saw these versatile birds perching on the balconies and cupolas of the City Palace (left), where they were likely hunting for small mammals or insects to satisfy their omnivorous appetites. Their light weight gives them an advantage over other scavengers. Because they do not need such strong updrafts to fly, they can start foraging in the early morning hours before the sun has fully warmed the air.

Like the kites, rose-ringed parakeets and red-wattled lapwings (below) were an accepted part of everyday life in Udaipur and other Indian cities. The parakeets darted like volleys of arrows over treetops in the parks and the lapwings etched their irregular wingbeats against the hot, blue sky before landing to feed near roadways and on open lawns.

The extroverted rose-ringed parakeet (above) is a favorite among some and a pest to others. They are kept as pets in cities and in villages, where they perch on their human companions' shoulders and are likely to provide more than enough parrot conversation. In the wild, they are just as playful—zipping through the air in small or large flocks, chasing each other and swooping down to investigate a wild fig tree or field of grain.

A VISIT TO BHARATPUR

Birgit and I were traveling down the main trail of the park at Bharatpur—a bird sanctuary southeast of Delhi. A slight breeze ruffled the leaves of the babul trees, and the waters of the *jheel* shimmered in the evening light. Pure white water lilies dotted the surrounding marshlands, and between their blooms I could just barely see a purple gallinule. Clad in Pre-Raphaelite purples and greens, it was picking its way across the lily pads, its toes spread out to distribute its weight over the floating leaves. In the painting above, I've shown a pair of these marsh birds scanning the landscape from the water's edge.

Flocks of pelicans, cormorants, spoonbills, and painted storks (right) were settling in for the night. The storks looked as if they had been dabbed with bits of leftover paint—orange-yellow for the bill and pink for the tops of their legs. From the back, their plumage looked like black and white dresses from Europe's *belle époque* drawn into a bustles, but from the front they had a starkly prehistoric look.

Anhingas were posing like pterodactyls on dead branches, and then there would be a blue flash and a jewel-like Eurasian kingfisher would perch there too. Our guides pointed out two different kinds of diminutive owls. As we traveled through this avian Eden, I remembered seeing two white Siberian cranes in the same place many years before, when I'd made my trip around the world. These birds are now rare, and their absence echoed all around us.

Robert Bateman 2002 ©

White-Throated Kingfisher and Least Grebe

For many years, the Bharatpur bird sanctuary was a duck-shooting ground. Its creator, the Maharajah of Bharatpur, had no intention of saving birds when he diverted water from an irrigation canal to create the freshwater marsh in the late nineteenth century. But conservationists later set aside the hunting preserve as a safe place for an abundant variety of wildlife, including spoonbills, cormorants, lily-trotting jacanas, wintering Siberian cranes, white-throated kingfishers (above), and least grebes (right).

When we left this enchanting realm, night was encroaching and the *jheel* was as quiet as a pause in a concerto, the babul trees reflected like tough-barked lace in its waters. Then came the cadenza to a perfect day as the sarus cranes settled down for the night—their calls echoing around the old hunting grounds that were now their sole domain.

Red Jungle Fowl and Peacock

The tangled growth and thorny thickets of India's tropical dry forests are tiger country, but travelers heading through these parts are sometimes astonished by the sound of a distinctly un-exotic "*Cock-a-doodle-do*" coming from beyond the bamboo stands. The call comes not from a rooster but from the ancestor of all roosters and chickens—the red jungle fowl (above). It is in the order Galliformes, which includes peafowl, as well as game birds like pheasants and partridges.

Although peacocks are at home in cities and temple grounds, where they were once kept to ward off snakes, many are also found where tigers dwell. Their excellent eyesight and hearing and speedy flight make them difficult to approach, but they are sometimes killed by leopards and eagles, as well as the stealthy tiger (right). I painted the male, overleaf, treading cautiously past temple ruins in a banyan grove, poised to run or fly to safety if he senses danger.

THE AFRICAN SAVANNA

I have always felt at home in the wild places of Africa. Even on my first trip, I sensed I was coming back to a place where people understood the wonderful complexities of the natural world because they observed them close up, every day. This drama has been most obvious on the savanna—the dry tropical and subtropical regions of the continent, where lions hide in the tousled grasses and giraffes browse on the branches of thorny acacia trees. And in these wild places, the lives of large mammals are also often connected with the birds that share their habitat. Ostriches in the Serengeti act as sentinels for feeding zebras, and crowned cranes capture insects stirred up by the hooves of cattle.

Some days, when we've gone on safari, the "big game" animals have not appeared, but with hornbills, flamingos, and sunbirds to study and rediscover, we have never been bored. Even in the settled regions, hundreds of multicolored species fly and forage in the parks, along roadsides, and in the secret corners of private gardens. And in East Africa, the acacia trees often bristle with the sounds of superb starlings sharing their perches with other birds (below). These brilliant blue-green birds are relatives of the common starling, which lives in northern countries. In the painting below, white-headed buffalo weavers and a pair of white-browed sparrow weavers are hidden in the branches behind.

When I was teaching in Nigeria in the 1960s, I took a trip east and encountered this unusual congregation of storks and egrets (right) moving silently across a stretch of savanna to northern Cameroon. The scene was remarkable for two reasons: these birds are more commonly found near water or in marshlands and it is rare to see them all together in a crowd. Saddle-billed storks (top left) use their vivid bills to harvest fish, though they do also forage on land. And the yellow-billed stork (middle right) often feeds at the edges of large bodies of water, using one foot to flush its prey out of the mud. But this slow-motion flock was foraging for grasshoppers and other ground-dwelling insects. In this painting, I gave the foreground to the sacred ibises, whose elegant symmetry was depicted in ancient Egyptian art.

Robert Bateman 2002

White-Bellied Bustard and Kori Bustard

Something was moving across the savanna and into my line of vision. I stopped sketching and reached for my binoculars. At first it was just a patch on the horizon, but in a few moments a stately bird with a softly tapered crest came into view. I was looking at a Kori bustard (left and below). Like its nature, the bustard's markings are restrained, except for a few brown splotches on its wings that look like material left over from another outfit. To me, it is this combination of subtlety and sleek nobility that makes a walking bustard an intriguing bird to paint.

The four-foot, forty-pound ground bird usually moves around by itself or in small flocks, and it rarely flies. It can't even perch, since it has no hind toe. Nevertheless, Kori bustards are enterprising feeders, supplementing their diet of locusts and seeds with termites, small mammals, and insects stuck in the gum of acacia trees. And at mating time, the male takes on the exuberance of a Romantic poet, fluffing up his elegant neck to four times its normal size, drooping his primaries so they touch the ground, and splaying his tail feathers to show off their white underpinnings. The great bustard goes one better, flipping his tail right over his back, sinking his head into his shoulders, and puffing out his neck so his head is almost completely hidden. The result is a billowing display that looks more like an inflated cauliflower than a bird!

Like all bustards, the Kori and the white-bellied bustard (above) hunt on the ground, and when they sense danger, they run, or if they fly, they cover only short distances. Because of these habits, they need extra warning to avoid predators, and the wide views of the open savanna are ideal for this purpose. Even these tactics do not save them from destruction at the hands of humans, however. All bustards lose feeding grounds when domestic animals are allowed to overgraze, and many are victimized by uncontrolled hunting in parts of Africa. Over a hundred years ago, similar killings eliminated the last great bustards in England.

Southern Ground Hornbill and Verreaux's Eagle Owl

One sun-baked day in the Serengeti, I came across this southern ground hornbill (left) standing like an oversized treble clef on the grass. These hornbills strut deliberately across the savanna, digging for insects with their spade-like bills and trying to stay clear of leopards, crocodiles, and baboons.

Like their red-billed relatives, ground hornbills build nests in tree holes or in rockface crevices, but the red-bills use more intriguing strategies for self-defense. The African savanna is a breeding ground for large raptors and puff adders just waiting to make dinner out of the hornbill's young, so the red-billed parents foil their enemies by sealing up their nest hole with mud, leftover bits of food, and droppings. The female works from the inside, using mud brought by the male, until she is completely walled in except for a small slit. The tiny crack acts like a window at a drive-through restaurant, and the male hornbill uses this opening to pass tasty grasshoppers and termites to his mate. She stays there for six weeks while she incubates the eggs and takes care of her brood. But when her oldest chick is about three weeks old, she breaks out of her confined quarters, using her strong bill to chip away at the mud wall that has now become as hard as brick.

The hornbill sports what are to me the most beautiful eyelashes in the animal kingdom.

We are always intrigued by the number of Verreaux's eagle owls we see in the big-game country of East Africa. On daytime safaris, we've often looked up into the trees and been rewarded by the sight of this bark-patterned bird looking back down at us and slowly blinking. The one I've painted here lived at Lake Nivasha in Kenya and belonged to Joy Adamson—the game warden's wife whose experiences in raising a lioness cub were dramatized in books and in the movie Born Free. This owl had also become somewhat tame under her care, but she was letting it live in the wild. In the evening, however, it always returned to be fed when she gave a particular call.

Egyptian and Lappet-Faced Vultures

We had started out in the cool hours before dawn, driving from the rim of Tanzania's Ngorongoro Crater to look for wildebeests. It was the birthing season and, ironically, one of the best ways to spot the newborn animals was to look for vultures circling over young that had been killed by waiting predators.

We passed through the waning darkness and on into the full light of the morning, coming at last to a streambank where a family of cheetahs was playing on the black volcanic soil. And not far away, there was a great commotion of vultures. We turned reluctantly from the cheetah family and drove on, taking our bearings from the position of the scavengers. They had, in fact, spotted a kill and were waiting impatiently while some juvenile lions finished their feast. As soon as the lions moved off, the vultures rushed in—along with a tawny eagle (right foreground) and a golden jackal. They were Egyptian vultures—one of the smallest of their kind— and they pecked delicately, using their curved beaks to get at the leftover tidbits.

Sometimes more massive vultures are the first to arrive at a kill, establishing a feeding hierarchy right from the beginning. The feast might be initiated by a lappet-faced vulture (above), which can tear through the hide of the carcass with its powerful bill. Once the larger bird has finished its meal, Egyptian vultures and tawny eagles move in to clean up the scraps.

Martial Eagle and Pygmy Falcon

We'd seen a pride of lions beyond the camp the night before, and we hoped to see them again as we drove out to the plain that morning. But something else was in store for us. As we wound our way among the fever trees, we noticed a castle-like tower of earth—one of the sculpted termite mounds that stand like earthen cairns on the savanna. Some small furry shapes were moving in the near distance, not too far from the mound, and we concluded that they must be banded mongooses (bottom right). These sleek mammals often live in termite colonies, where they find ready-made homes in the tunnels that ventilate the tower. In this ingenious dwelling, they also enjoy the side benefit of lunching on their termite neighbors.

We had just decided that the mongooses were coming back from a hunting expedition when suddenly they started to run. We thought we'd startled them, so we prepared to drive off and leave them in peace. Just then a martial eagle (left) swooped down from the sky, its eight-foot wingspread casting a shadow over the band of foragers. With its keen eyesight, the bird may have noticed them even through the tangled branches of the trees. Whatever the source of its information, it had now found a ready feast. It stretched out its long feathered legs and huge black claws and grabbed one of the little creatures while the others disappeared from sight. The victim was seized by the head and taken away, dangling from the raptor's talons and shrouded in its shadow. Following the eagle's trail, we drove over hummocks and among fallen trunks and eventually found the bird perched on the limb of a fever tree, preparing to devour its lifeless prey.

The pygmy falcon (above) is about the size of an American robin, but like the martial eagle, it is a raptor and a ruthless hunter. These deceptively soft-feathered birds perch on exposed branches to catch sight of smaller birds or insects, which it captures in mid-air. Like many creatures, pygmy falcons live in a symbiotic, or mutually beneficial, relationship with another bird species—the white-headed buffalo weaver. They move into abandoned weavers' nests and, in return, it's thought that the falcons' aggressive behavior protects the other weavers in the tree from predators.

Robert Bateman 2001©

Crowned Crane

Melting snows from Mount Kilimanjaro feed into streams that provide water for a panoply of wildlife, including elephants, pelicans, giraffes, impalas, and kingfishers. One evening, I was coming back after many hours of watching these animals and I thought the wonders of the day were complete. But as I passed a stand of acacias, I looked up to see the most memorable vision of those hours—a pair of crowned cranes flying in their slow, deliberate way toward the trees. The sun was setting, but it was impossible to miss the aristocratic four-foot birds as they glided toward the topmost branches to rest.

Then a full moon came up—and the two cranes stood gracefully above that circle of light, their crowns of golden fireworks still faintly visible, like living haiku written onto the fabric of the African night (left).

Like crowned cranes, blues have a deliciously exuberant courtship. Both partners first dance in a circle, then stop and call gracefully in unison. After this elegant prelude, total mayhem breaks loose as the cranes throw grass into the air and jump to great heights with their wings flapping—then kick at clumps of grass or whatever they encounter as they flutter back down to the ground (below).

Blue Crane

I've always seen the blue crane's plumage as a lyrical counterpoint to the operatic flash and verve of the crowned crane. Though the tail feathers of the male blue swoop down dramatically, his body plumes are a uniform slate-blue-gray and the female's feathers are even more subdued, with a tinge of russet on the back. The crane in the painting above is wading into a pool of water to roost there for the night. In a few minutes, he may be joined by a heron or stork. Most of the time, however, blue cranes stay away from the water, feeding almost exclusively in South Africa's rolling upland velds.

Greater and Lesser Flamingos

We drove as close as we dared on the salt-encrusted floodplain of the lake. If we moved ahead just a bit, we would get a good view of the feeding flamingos, but we did not want to frighten them away—and we especially did not want to break through the crust into the slimy mud below. To the naked eye, the birds looked like a rosy mirage floating above the reddish waters of Lake Magadi. But with the telephoto I could zoom in on the crook-tipped bills of a single pair as they dredged the mud, looking for dinner. The lanky water birds kept up a continuous conversational babble as they fed, saying "*Kuk-kuk, ke-kuk; kuk-kuk, ke-kuk*"—but they did not notice us hidden at the edge of their feeding ground.

Lake Magadi lies at the very bottom of Tanzania's Ngorongoro Crater—within the Great Rift Valley that is slowly but surely pulling Africa apart. It is fed by a hot spring that bubbles up through old volcanic rocks, dissolving sulfates and carbonates, which cool and crystallize at the surface. Humans would burn their throats if they tried to drink those waters, but flamingos are equipped with salt-secreting glands that protect them as they feed. Two flamingo species thrive in the soda-encrusted Lake Magadi: the lesser flamingo (left), which is about two and a half feet tall and has a dark bill, and the greater flamingo (above), which is twice that height and has only a black tip on its bill. They manage to live together because they feed on different organisms. Greater flamingos use their legs to stir up brine shrimp and mollusks from the lake's mud-water flats; lesser flamingos thrive on a blue-green algae called spirulina. Both species use their large fleshy tongues to press their catch against the lamellae, or filters, at the edges of their bills, straining out the mud and water and gobbling up the algae or shrimp.

This diet affects the color of the flamingos' feathers. When first hatched, the birds are fluffy white, and as fledglings, they are a nondescript gray. But the carotenoids in their food eventually create the famous coral hues of the flamingos' adult plumage.

When the rains are sparse, salt lakes dry up, and the flamingos feeding in them must either trek overland to another lake or die. I have never seen this mass exodus, but in 1971, thirty thousand birds walked north from Namibia's Etosha Pan to a lake eighteen miles away. Then that lake dried up and the birds were forced to march another twenty-five miles to a steady water supply. Many perished en route, but even more would have died had they stayed where they'd been.

Even at a stable lake, flamingo chicks fall victim to their harsh environment. At times, the soda deposits in alkaline lakes form anklets around their legs, becoming so heavy that the young can no longer move, so they are left to die.

Red Bishop

It's not unusual to see legendary species like cranes, eagles, and storks against the African sky, but these azure spaces are also punctuated by the flights of smaller birds. The red bishop (right) is a member of the weaver family, which includes the social weavers of southern Africa. Those tiny birds build huge communal nests weighing as much as several tons, but the male red bishop constructs a much neater, compact globe-shaped nest—often slung between reeds. When two or three females appear, he takes his position on one of the reed stems and puffs himself up to twice his normal size. Or he may try to get their attention by launching into a bee-like flight and rapidly beating his wings.

Scarlet-Chested Sunbird

I've shown the scarlet-chested sunbird to the left sipping nectar from a leonotis—a plant that grows in many parts of lion country. Like all sunbirds, this bird has a downpointed bill, perfectly suited to fishing nectar out of deep-petaled flowers. If that doesn't work, the bird will stab the petals at the base to release its meal.

Eurasian Roller

The lilac-breasted roller is one of the most common rollers in big-game country, but the bird at the right is a Eurasian roller, which has migrated to Africa for the winter months. Some Eurasian rollers travel up to six thousand miles over ocean and desert to escape the frosts of the northern hemisphere.

I've shown the bird opposite in a typical pose—resting on a whistling thorn covered with sphere-shaped galls. Created by ants as nesting places, the galls actually bring the tree some benefit. Any creature that tries to eat part of a branch risks being stopped by a swarm of biting ants!

For Paul & Betty Rae with best wishes and happy memories. Robert Bateman 2001

TO THE ANTARCTIC

Wandering Alb

As we headed for South Georgia Island, our ship rolled and pitched over heavy swells. Anyone who could tolerate being on deck was clinging to the rails with one hand and holding onto their binoculars with the other, staring into the raging waves to catch sight of whatever oceangoing (pelagic) birds they could see in the lurching landscape. A royal albatross floated like a glider just above the water (above) using the updrafts displaced by the waves to stay aloft, and delicate little storm petrels hovered over the ocean, flitting just out of reach of the churning sea.

We finally landed on the leeward side of a small island near South Georgia, where the wandering albatross were known to nest, and from there, we climbed up a small river to their colony. On the windward side of this desolate no-man's-land, we found the birds sitting contentedly under the drizzling rain. They had to live on this wind-lashed promontory because they needed its air currents and cliff height to launch themselves into the air. Like hang gliders, albatross have disproportionately long wings, which give them more lift—but the birds' aerodynamic pièce de résistance is the structure in their bones that keeps their wings in "spread-out" position. With that lock in place, albatross can keep their wings open for long periods of time without using much muscle power.

Like its companions, the nesting bird to the right was entirely unafraid as I came up close to sketch the streamlined interlocking facets of its bill. It merely observed me in its placid way, like a noble courtier receiving the envoys of a foreign monarch.

5.5 Albatross Island, South Georgia, Jan. 25/99 — Robert Bateman —

King Penguin

To me, the peaks of South Georgia Island in the Antarctic seas are even more awe-inspiring than the Swiss Alps or the North American Rockies. Their glaciers stretch right down to the ocean, making a jagged pattern against the Delft-blue mountains. I knew this Subantarctic region was rich in wildlife, but I didn't realize the extent of its abundance and diversity until I actually visited the island. South Georgia's capes and bays were filled with colonies of breeding birds, and sea lions loped along the beach. The island is surrounded by oxygen-rich waters, which, when combined with the strong summer sunlight, create a continual population explosion of plankton and shrimp-like krill. These little crustaceans, in turn, provide food for South Georgia's huge king penguin populations. Without them, the birds could not survive.

Our trek to the penguin colony seemed to take forever, but the penguins themselves walk that distance every day bringing food back for their growing young. As we approached the nesting ground, we heard the birds first, making their strident cries and squabbling among themselves. Then we were assaulted by a wall of fishy guano smells—a precursor to the sight of thousands and thousands of three-foot-high birds standing among pebbly rivulets and clumps of grass like a crowd on a market square. Each nest was spaced at pecking distance from the others, so from the air, they would have looked like a pattern of uniformly spaced polka dots. From a closer vantage point, the individual adults resembled softly sculpted versions of Georgia O'Keeffe paintings, with their silver-gray backs and wings and cleanly curved orange-yellow highlights (right). But their offspring were dressed in frowzled brown, as if they were wrapped in overstuffed raccoon coats (left).

King Penguin Chicks Jan. 24/96
Fortuna Bay, South Georgia   Robert Bateman

Humans are accustomed to being noticed by wildlife, and especially by birds. But here we did not arouse the least bit of interest! As we stood in the middle of the busy penguin intersections, the adults brushed past us without stopping—much too absorbed in their everyday business to worry about a few stray homo sapiens. *Parent penguins are always hard at work, because it takes three years for each pair to raise two chicks, and for a good part of that time, the young cannot fish on their own. Their feathers are not waterproof and they have not yet acquired the inch or so of fat needed to insulate them from the icy Antarctic waters. So the adults spend many hours walking out to sea, catching fish or krill, and hiking back to the colony to feed their young.*

164

Chinstrap Penguin and Gentoo Penguin

We'd landed on Deception Island, a dormant volcano at the very tip of the peninsula that juts out of the Antarctic mainland, dividing the Atlantic from the Pacific Ocean. Ahead of us stood a massive mountain whose pinkish-gray terrain was marked with white dots that became smaller and smaller the higher you looked. It was one vast city of tens of thousands of chinstrap penguins stretching up toward the sky. Strangely enough, chinstraps view the highest spots as the best pieces of real estate, even though they're farthest from the birds' fishing grounds. These locations are attractive because they're most exposed to the sun and are therefore the first to warm up in the spring. A head start like this is a distinct advantage to any penguin, whose young need all the time they can get to grow up before the onset of the Antarctic winter.

The beach where we landed also happened to be the penguins' main thoroughfare for going back and forth to the sea, so we observed penguin etiquette and were careful not to block their route. To do the sketches for the painting to the right, I sat down on the beach next to the line and let them flow around me, like a stream around a boat.

This gentoo chick (above) looks quite cozy as the first snowflakes of winter cluster on his downy coat. But the scene may have a tragic ending. Since the young bird does not yet have his waterproof feathers, he may not be ready to follow his parents to sea before full freeze-up. Yet if he stays on land, he'll have no fish to eat and will starve.

Giant Petrel and Leucistic Gentoo Penguin

Most petrels behave like albatross, soaring above the ocean for hours at a time. But southern giant petrels can also walk around on land quite comfortably. On the Antarctic Peninsula, we saw these two giants using their walking skills to bully a solitary leucistic gentoo penguin. (Leucistics are like albinos, but they have some dark markings.) Like most albinos and leucistics, this bird was an easy

Robert Bateman 2000 ©

target for predators, which tend to attack anything that looks different and may therefore be sick or weak. But the little penguin put up a good fight, keeping its beak open, ready to peck at the petrels' wings. Eventually the bullies gave up their sport and flew away. Southern giant petrels are circumpolar—they inhabit territories all around the Pole—and they prey on birds and animals on land and sea. They are also the "vultures" of this region, cleaning up the landscape by scavenging on carrion. Unfortunately, they often follow long-line fishing vessels, and like the albatross, they meet their deaths entangled in bait hooks. As a result, populations of petrels and albatross are dwindling in many regions.

Emperor Penguins Cape Washington Dec 4.   Robert Bateman 2001

Emperor Penguin

Icebergs shone opalescent under the rays of the midnight sun as we arrived at the emperor colony near Cape Washington. Twice as heavy as the king penguins of South Georgia, emperors live and nest on sheer ice, and the males incubate their eggs in the darkest days of the Antarctic winter.

In May or June the female emperor lays her egg, but only hours later she must go to sea for much-needed meals of krill. So she leaves the male to do the incubation work, holding the egg on top of his feet under a warm pouch. Even as the winds reach speeds of a hundred miles an hour, the egg stays warmer than its harsh surroundings by eighty degrees centigrade. But the insulation on the rest of the father-bird's body is not as effective, so the males gather and huddle close together in the increasing darkness, the crowd continually shifting so the penguins on the outside do not freeze. By the time the chicks hatch, their long-suffering protectors are nearly starved but cannot look for food until their mates return. Only then can the heroic fathers begin the long trek to sea to catch their first meal in nearly four months.

Since they live on ice and snow, emperors have two traveling methods: waddling upright and scooting up and down hills like toboggans (above). During our midnight visit to their domain, they kept up this exuberant play, their feathers glinting gold in the never-ending sunset.

Adélie Penguin

It was nearly Christmas when we entered the "deep south" of the Antarctic and discovered a colony of Adélie penguins. Since all Adélies have the same classic "tuxedo-waiter" look, it is sometimes difficult to tell the sexes apart, but this time it was easy. The males were the ones dropping pebbles on the ground, trying to gain the affections of their prospective mates (below). At first, the female will fight her suitor, but the conflict is short if she is interested, and the two will then begin gathering more rocks to build their nest. Pebbles are valued commodities in Adélie colonies because they are used to construct well-drained nests high above the wet muck of the surrounding ground. The partly grown chick at right is keeping dry by resting on another rocky perch.

Index to the Paintings and Drawings

63 (bottom) *Three Mallard Chicks*, 1993
4" x 6"; acrylic on mylar

64 *Burrowing Owl Study*, 1988
6 ½" x 9"; mixed media on board

65 *Prairie Falcon and Prey*, 2001
20" x 16"; acrylic on board

66 *Baltimore Oriole and Willow*, 1994*
10" x 8"; original lithograph

67 (top) *Rose-Breasted Grosbeak Singing*, 2002
10" x 8 ¼"; mixed media on paper

67 (bottom) *Canada Warbler and Pear Blossoms*, 1999*
6 ⅞" x 11 ⅞"; acrylic on board

68 *Scarlet Tanager and Alder Blossoms*, 1999*
6 ⅞" x 11 ⅞"; acrylic on board

69 (left) *Blackburnian Warbler*, 2002
11" x 8 ½"; mixed media on paper

69 (right) *Black-Throated Green Warbler*, 2001
10" x 6 ½"; acrylic on canvas

70 *Lucas Porch*, 2000*
36" x 36"; acrylic on canvas

71 (top) *Robins at the Nest*, 1985*
12" x 16"; acrylic on board

71 (bottom) *Baby Robin*, 2002
5 ¼" x 7 ⅜"; acrylic on mylar

72 *Gatekeeper*, 2001*
11 ⅞" x 17"; acrylic on board

72-73 *Cliff Swallows at Nest*, 2001
8 ⅞" x 11 ⅞"; acrylic on board

74-75 *The Immigrants*, 1987*
17 ¼" x 23 ½"; acrylic on board

75 (top) *Young Starling*, 2002
6 ⅞" x 10"; acrylic on canvas

75 (bottom) *Rock Doves*, 2002
7" x 10"; acrylic on mylar

76 *Ring-Necked Pheasant Crowing*, 2001
11 ⅛" x 11 ¾"; acrylic on board

77 *Pheasant in Cornfield*, 1978*
22" x 26"; acrylic on board

78 *Vesper Sparrow on Fencepost*, 2002
10 ⅛" x 7 ¼"; mixed media on paper

79 *Summer Song—Bobolink*, 2001*
20" x 16"; acrylic on board

80 *Turkey Vulture*, 1991
11" x 14"; mixed media on paper

81 *Turkey Vulture in Dead Elm*, 1967
35" x 37"; acrylic on board

82 *Red-Tailed Hawk on Willow*, 1971
48" x 40"; acrylic on board

83 *Red-Tailed Hawk on Fencepost*, 1971
22 ¼" x 28 ¼"; acrylic on board

84 *Kestrel*, 1994
15 ¾" x 10 ½"; watercolor on paper

85 (top left) *Buteo sketch*, 2002
7 ½" x 4 ½"; pen on paper

85 (top middle) *Falcon sketch*, 2002
7" x 5 ¼"; pen on paper

85 (top right) *Accipiter sketch*, 2002
7" x 6 ¼"; pen on paper

85 (bottom) *Goshawk Head*, 1978
6 ½" x 9 ¾"; acrylic on board

86 *Saw-Whet Owl and Mouse*, 1979
11 ½" x 8"; mixed media on paper

87 *Screech Owl in Apple Tree*, 2001*
10 ⅛" x 12"; gouache on board

88 *Samantha*, 2000*
12" x 16"; mixed media on board

89 *Winter Mist—Great Horned Owl*
(detail), 1970*
38" x 29"; acrylic on masonite

90 *Downy Woodpecker Study*, 2001*
5 ⅞" x 5 ⅞"; acrylic on board

90-91 *Hairy Woodpecker and Birch*, 2001*
11 ⅞" x 17"; acrylic on board

92 *Flying Pileated Woodpecker*, 2002
4 ⅞" x 7"; pen on paper

93 *Pileated Woodpecker Pair on White Pine*, 2001
11 ⅝" x 12"; acrylic on board

94 *Canada Geese over Escarpment* (detail), 1984
10" x 13"; mixed media on paper

94-95 *Mill Pond—Canada Geese*, 1997*
19" x 25"; acrylic on board

96 *Winter Cattails—Red-Winged Blackbird*, 1997*
18" x 12"; acrylic on board

97 *Female Red-Winged Blackbird*, 2002
7" x 11"; pen on paper

98 *Lunging Heron*, 1988*
11" x 20"; acrylic on board

98-99 *Wading Heron and Willow*, 1998*
16" x 20"; acrylic on board

100-101 *Loon Gathering at Big East*, 2001*
30" x 60"; acrylic on canvas

101 *Loon Stretching*, 2002
10 ⅛" x 7 ¼"; mixed media on paper

102 *Puffin and Gull Colony*, 2001
15" x 12"; acrylic on canvas

102-103 *Gull and Puffin*, 2001
16" x 18"; acrylic on board

104-105 *Gannet Greeting*, 2001
9" x 10"; acrylic on board

105 *Gannet Colony*, 2001
7 ½" x 5"; acrylic on board

106 *Roseate Spoonbill*, 2001
24" x 24"; acrylic on board

107 *Black Skimmers*, 2001
6 ⅝" x 13 ⅜"; acrylic on canvas

108 *Brown Pelicans Preening*, 2001
6 ½" x 15 ⅛"; acrylic on board

109 *Brown Pelicans*, 2001
24" x 24"; acrylic on board

110 *Egret Congregation*, 2000
7 ⅞" x 12"; acrylic on board

111 *Great Egrets Fighting*, 2001
48" x 48"; acrylic on canvas

112 (top) *Collared Aracari*, 2002
8 ½" x 11"; mixed media on paper

112 (bottom) *Keel-Billed Toucan*, 2002
8 ½" x 11"; mixed media on paper

113 *Parrots at Claybank*, 2001
13 ¼" x 16"; acrylic on canvas

114-115 *Tropical Canopy—Scarlet Macaws*, 2001*
20" x 36"; acrylic on board

116 *Frigatebirds Flying*, 2002
8 ½" x 11"; mixed media on paper

116-117 *Magnificent Frigatebird*, 2001
10" x 16"; acrylic on board

118 *Yellow-Crowned Night Herons*, 1991
15" x 12"; acrylic on board

119 (top) *Red-Footed Booby*, 1981
16" x 20"; acrylic on board

119 (bottom) *Blue-Footed Boobies*, 2001
6 ⅞" x 15 ⅛"; acrylic on board

120 *Irish Church and Barn Owl*, 1999*
36" x 36"; acrylic on canvas

121 *Bullfinch and Berries*, 2001
7 ⅞" x 15 ⅞"; acrylic on board

122 *Blue Tits and Great Tit*, 2001
8" x 12"; acrylic on canvas

123 (top) *Eurasian Blackbird*, 2002
8 3/16" x 9 ½"; acrylic on upo

123 (bottom) *European Robin*, 2002
6" x 8"; acrylic on mylar

124-125 *House Martins and Gargoyles*, 1996
10" x 18 ⅜"; gouache and oil on board

125 *Avocet Portrait*, 1996
8" x 6"; gouache and oil on board

126 *Red Crossbill Pair in Pine*, 2001
12" x 10"; acrylic on board

127 (left) *Alpine Chough*, 1996
8" x 6"; gouache and oil on board

127 (right) *Dipper at Rocky Shore*, 1996
16" x 12"; gouache and alkyd on mylar

128-129 *Capercaillie* (detail), 1992
12" x 24"; acrylic on masonite

129 *Capercaillie sketch*, 1988
7" x 5"; pencil on paper

130 *European Kingfisher*, 2001
7 1/2" x 9 3/8"; acrylic on paper

130-131 *Black Woodpecker*, 2001
9" x 12"; acrylic on board

132 *Lammergeier at Nest*, 2001
14 5/8" x 15 5/8"; acrylic on paper

132-133 *Lammergeier Vulture*, 2001
12" x 20"; acrylic on board

134 *Three Swan Heads*, 1994
4" x 5 1/2"; acrylic on mylar

134-135 *Bank of Swans*, 1999*
18 1/8" x 36"; acrylic on board

136 *Taj with Birdlife*, 2001
12" x 13"; acrylic on canvas

137 (top) *Laggar Falcon and Taj*, 2001
11 3/4" x 22 1/2"; acrylic on canvas

137 (bottom) *Hoopoes*, 2001
5 1/8" x 12"; acrylic on mylar

138 *Black Kites at Udaipur*, 2001
16" x 20"; acrylic on board

139 (top) *Rose-Ringed Parakeet*, 2001
5 3/4" x 12"; acrylic on canvas

139 (bottom) *Red-Wattled Lapwing*, 2001
11" x 10 1/2"; acrylic on board

140 *Purple Gallinules*, 2001
10" x 7"; acrylic on board

141 *Painted Storks*, 2001
24" x 24"; acrylic on board

142 (top) *White-Throated Kingfisher*, 2001
5 5/8" x 11 3/8"; acrylic on mylar

142 (bottom) *Least Grebe*, 2001
7 1/2" x 10"; acrylic on board

143 (top) *Red Jungle Fowl*, 2001
9" x 12"; acrylic on board

143 (bottom) *Tiger sketch*, 2001
1 3/4" x 4"; pen on paper

144-145 *Banyan Walk— Peacock*, 2001*
24" x 42"; acrylic on canvas

146 *Superb Starlings in Acacia Tree*, 2001
9" x 11 7/8"; acrylic on canvas

147 *Savanna Birds*, 2001
16" x 16"; acrylic on board

148 *Kori Bustard Displaying*, 2001
9 5/8" x 9 7/8"; acrylic on canvas

149 (left) *Kori Bustard*, 2002
8" x 10"; mixed media on paper

149 (right) *White-Bellied Bustard*, 1981
10" x 6"; acrylic on board

150 (left) *Ground Hornbill*, 1997*
20" x 16"; oil on board

150 (right) *Ground Hornbill study*, 2002
5 1/2" x 7"; pencil on paper

151 *Giant Eagle Owl*, 1997
20" x 16"; oil on board

152 *Lappet-Faced Vulture*, 1997
19 1/2" x 15 3/4"; pencil on paper

152-153 *Carrion Crew*, 2001
12" x 24"; acrylic on board

154 *Euphorbia Tree and Martial Eagle*, 1999
36" x 36"; acrylic on canvas

155 (left) *Martial Eagle and Mongoose Kill*, 2002
8 1/2" x 11"; mixed media on paper

155 (right) *Pygmy Falcon*, 1997*
20" x 16"; oil on board

155 (bottom) *Martial Eagle and Mongooses* (detail), 2002
8 1/2" x 11"; mixed media on paper

156 *Crowned Cranes and Moon*, 2001
24" x 24"; acrylic on board

157 (left) *Blue Cranes Dancing*, 2002
7" x 11"; pen on paper

157 (right) *Blue Crane Wading*, 2001
15 1/2" x 15 1/2"; acrylic on board

158 *Flamingos Feeding*, 2001
12" x 12"; acrylic on board

159 *Flamingos at Ngorongoro (detail)*, 2001
30" x 40"; acrylic on canvas

160 (left) *Scarlet-Chested Sunbird*, 2001
10" x 5 5/8"; acrylic on mylar

160 (right) *Red Bishop*, 2001
8 1/2" x 5"; acrylic on board

161 *Eurasian Roller on Whistling Thorn*, 2001
8 1/2" x 11 3/4"; acrylic on canvas

162 *Wandering Albatross and Wave*, 2001
3 3/4" x 10 1/2"; acrylic on paper

162-163 *Wandering Albatross*, 1998
5 3/4" x 9 1/4"; mixed media on paper

164 (top) *King Penguin Chicks*, 1998
5 3/4" x 4 3/4"; mixed media on paper

164 (bottom) *King Penguin Study*, 1985
6" x 10 3/4"; pencil on paper

165 *Ecstatic Display—King Penguins*, 2001
13 3/4" x 12"; acrylic on mylar

166 *Juvenile Gentoo Penguin in Snow*, 2001
11 3/8" x 16 3/4"; acrylic on canvas

167 *Chinstrap Parade*, 2001
11" x 8 1/2"; acrylic on canvas

168-169 *Giant Petrels and Albino Gentoo Penguin*, 1999
20" x 48"; acrylic on canvas

170 (top) *Emperor Penguins Sliding*, 2001
3 3/4" x 10 1/2"; acrylic on paper

170 (bottom) *Emperor Penguin and Chick*, 2001
7" x 4 5/8"; pen on paper

171 (left) *Adélie with Pebble*, 2002
8 1/2" x 11"; mixed media on paper

171 (right) *Adélie Chick*, 1998
5 3/4" x 4 3/4"; mixed media on paper

176 *Tawny Owl Nap*, 2000
7" x 5"; mixed media on paper

---

* These works, as well as other paintings by Robert Bateman, have been published as limited edition prints on paper and/or canvas by Mill Pond Press. For more information about their print publishing program, please direct inquiries to the appropriate address:

In the United States:

The Mill Pond Press Companies
310 Center Court
Venice, FL 34292-3500
941-497-6020
www.millpond.com

In Canada:

Nature's Scene
91 Armstrong Avenue
Georgetown, Ontario L7G 4S1
905-702-9116
www.naturesscene.com

In the United Kingdom:

Solomon & Whitehead Limited
Lynn Lane, Shenstone
Lichfield, Staffordshire WS14 0DX
44-1543-480696
www.fineartgroup.co.uk

Bibliography

Aristotle. *Generation of Animals.* Translated by A.L. Peck. Cambridge, MA, and London: Harvard University Press and William Heinemann, 1963.

Aristotle. *Parts of Animals.* Translated by A.L. Peck. Cambridge, MA, and London: Harvard University Press and William Heinemann, 1961.

Attenborough, David. *The Life of Birds.* Princeton, NJ: Princeton University Press, 1998.

Audubon, Maria R. *Audubon and His Journals.* Vol. 1. New York: Dover, 1986. (Original publication: New York: Scribner's, 1897.)

Barber, Theodore Xenophon. *The Human Nature of Birds.* New York: St. Martin's Press, 1993.

Flegg, Jim, ed. *Birds of the British Isles.* London: Orbis, 1984.

Gill, Frank B. *Ornithology.* New York: W.H. Freeman, 1990.

Gooders, John, and Scott Weidensaul, eds. *The Practical Ornithologist.* New York: Simon and Schuster, 1990.

Kaufman, Kenn. *Lives of North American Birds.* Boston: Houghton Mifflin, 1996.

Lansdowne, J.F. *Birds of the West Coast.* Vol. 1. Toronto: M.F. Feheley, 1976.

Lindblad, Lisa, and Sven-Olof. *The Serengeti: Land of Endless Space.* New York: Rizzoli International Publications, Inc., 1989.

Line, Les, and Franklin Russell. *The Audubon Society Book of Wild Birds.* New York: Harry N. Abrams, 1976.

Pearson, T. Gilbert, editor-in-chief. *Birds of America.* New York: Garden City Publishing Company, Inc., 1936.

Peterson, Roger Tory. *A Field Guide to the Birds of Eastern and Central North America.* Boston: Houghton Mifflin, 1980.

Peterson, Roger Tory. *A Field Guide to Western Birds.* 2nd ed. 1941; Boston: Houghton Mifflin, 1961.

Pettingill, Olin Sewall, Jr. *Ornithology in Laboratory and Field.* 5th ed. Illustrated by Walter J. Breckenridge. Orlando: Academic Press, 1985.

Poole, Robert M., ed. *The Wonder of Birds.* Washington, DC: The National Geographic Society, 1983.

Rising, Trudy, and Jim Rising. *Canadian Songbirds and Their Ways,* illustrated by Kathryn DeVos-Miller. Montreal: Tundra Books, 1982.

Russell, Franklin. *The Sea Has Wings,* photographs by Les Line. New York: Dutton, 1973.

Savage, Candace. *The Wonder of Canadian Birds.* Saskatoon, Saskatchewan: Western Producer Prairie Books, 1985.

Scott, Peter, ed. *The World Atlas of Birds.* New York: Crescent Books, 1974.

Steyn, Peter. *Nesting Birds: The Breeding Habits of Southern African Birds.* Vlaeberg: Fernwood Press, 1996.

Stuart, Chris and Tilde. *Birds of Africa: From Seabirds to Seed-Eaters.* Cambridge, MA: The MIT Press, 1999.

Symons, R.D. *Hours and the Birds: A Saskatchewan Record.* Toronto: University of Toronto Press, 1967.

Terres, John K. *The Audubon Society Encyclopedia of North American Birds.* New York: Alfred A. Knopf, 1980.

Wynne-Edwards, Vero Copner. *Seabirds of Percé and the Gaspé Peninsula,* 4th ed. Montreal: Mercury Press, 1954.

Websites Consulted

Acorn woodpecker:
- http://animaldiversity.ummz.umich.edu/accounts/melanerpes/m._formicivorus$narrative.html
- http://www.santaritalodge.com/BirdSpecs/Acorn%20Woodpecker.htm

Burrowing owl:
- http://rbcm1.rbcm.gov.bc.ca/end_species/species/burowl.html
- www.natureask/obo.htm
- http://members.aol.com/_ht_a/owlwebsite/burrow1/index.html?mtbrand=AOL_US

Cattle egret:
- http://www.nwf.org/internationalwildlife/egrets.html

European dipper:
- http://www.bartleby.com/65/di/dipper.html

European robin:
- www.1dolphin.org/muchmusic.html

Harris's hawk:
- http://ccwild.cbi.tamucc.edu/naturalhistory/harris'_hawk/hrshacc.htm

Lammergeier vulture:
- http://www.vultures.homestead.com/Bearded~main.html

Puffin:
- www.audubon.org/bird/puffin/what.html

Pygmy falcon:
- http://sandiegozoo.com/wildideas/animal/birds_of_prey.html

Raven:
- www.univie.ac.at/zoology/nbs/gruenau/ravens.html

Red crossbill:
- http://birds.cornell.edu/bow/REDCRO/

Redhead:
- http://duckcentral.com/redhead.html

Red-legged kittiwake:
- www.worldwildlife.org/wildworld/profiles/terrestrial/na/na1102_full.html

Ruffed grouse:
- www.ruffedgrousesociety.org/Version1/ruff.htm

Sandhill crane:
- http://www.pbs.org/audubon/wildwings/sandhillcrane.html

Santa Rita Mountains:
- http://209.238.248.22/maderacanyon.html

Swan:
- http://sites.state.pa.us/PA_Exec/PGC/swan/history.htm

Western scrub jay:
- http://birds.cornell.edu/BOW/WSCJAY
- http://207.34.92.247/birdsite/brdpgs/480.htm

Acknowledgments

For almost as long as I can remember, birds and the works of Robert Bateman have graced my life with their wildness and intricate artistry. So my first and heartfelt thanks go to Bob for inspiring me to honor and love the natural world, even before I had the privilege of collaborating with him on this book. The creation of *Birds* was a team effort, beginning with a series of interviews I had with Bob while he was on tour in what I've always known as "Bateman country"—the farms and woodlots of Halton County, west of Toronto. As we drove through those November fields, his awareness of the lives of birds became immediately apparent as he taught me how to spot red-tailed hawks perched on hydro poles and shared his encyclopedic knowledge of the habits and esthetic appeal of birds that he has seen around the world. As the book evolved, Bob also sent me written excerpts of his recollections of many more birding adventures and created a gallery of original works of art, most of which are appearing in this volume for the first time.

Bob's wife, Birgit, also offered me her detailed knowledge of birds and gave accounts of journeys she and Bob have taken together. Thank you, Birgit, for those important additions.

A special thank you also goes to Alex Fischer, executive assistant *extraordinaire*, for fielding questions with wit and wise perspective and for orchestrating the assembly of art on a global scale. And thank you also to Kate Carson, Bateman studio assistant, who patiently handled so many of my picayune requests.

Numerous experts provided me with inside information and vivid anecdotes about the world of birds and birders, and some checked accounts for accuracy (any inaccuracies that remain are my own): Ysbrand Brouwers, The Netherlands—Founder and Artistic Director, Artists for Nature Foundation; Dr. Bristol Foster, British Columbia; Dr. Al Gordon, Ontario; Ron Ridout, Long Point Bird Observatory, Bird Studies Canada; Mark C. Ross, Denver, Colorado, and Kenya—Author and Safari Guide; and Frederick (Derick) J. Watson, St. Abbs, Scotland, Artist.

Other experts from all over the world gave me special guidance during the first stages of research: Peter Alden, Concord, Massachusetts, Naturalist, Author and Lecturer; Dr. George Archibald, International Crane Foundation, Baraboo, Wisconsin; K. David Bishop, Australia, Ornithologist; R. Wayne Campbell, Curator of Ornithology, Royal British Columbia Museum; Dick Cannings, British Columbia, Consulting Biologist; Victor Emanuel, Victor Emanuel Nature Tours, Austin, Texas; Tom Gullick, Spain; Kay McKeever, The Owl Foundation, Ontario; Mark and Christine Read, Everard Read Gallery, Johannesburg, South Africa; Jordi Sargatal, Barcelona—Fondacion Territori I Paisatge, President de la Institucio Catalan d'Historia Natural, and member of the Editorial Council for the *Handbook of Birds of the World*; Raj Singh, India—co-author of *A Birdwatcher's Guide to India*; and Gustave J. Yaki, Calgary, Alberta—Naturalist and Tour Leader.

Special thank-yous go to Hamish Robertson for his efficient research and to Evelyn Mackie for her assistance in the early phases of this book. And my particular gratitude goes to V. John Lee, equally at home with words and images, for his intelligent good humor and elegant book design.

The staff at Madison Press already know how much I have benefited from their guidance. I am grateful to Hugh Brewster, Editorial Director, whose vision and personal care brought refinement and balance to this project, and to Sandra Hall, Production Manager, whose superb production expertise and composure under fire are gratefully appreciated. My thanks also go to Susan Aihoshi, Managing Editor, for her unfailing support, and to Lloyd Davis, for his perceptive copy editing. And, finally, there is Mireille Majoor, Editor *sans pareille*, who tempered my initial flights of research fancy with her legendary tact and good sense and transformed a set of disparate words and works of art into a book that soars.

I would also like to thank the people who first gave me a love for the land and for the lives of birds: the Native people of Niagara, a farmer who knew the beauty of wild swans, one extraordinary pilot, and my family, for many splendid moments spent watching birds from our northeast kitchen window. And finally, to the birds, I give thanks for their often inspiring ways and their ability to live full lives at the edge of danger.

Kathryn Dean
Toronto, Ontario, May 2002

BIRDS was produced by Madison Press Books